Sermon Illustrations of the Bible

TOPICALLY ARRANGED

❦

By KEITH L. BROOKS

Author of The Summarized Bible; Perplexing Passages
in the Four Gospels; Prophecies of Daniel
and Revelation; and Various
Bible Study Booklets

———

———

Published by
BIBLE INSTITUTE OF LOS ANGELES
536-558 South Hope Street
Los Angeles, California

A Word to Ministers and Bible Teachers

IT IS quite a general complaint these days among church attendants that too many sermons are merely philosophical and scientific dissertations, or merely literary productions.

The sermons that have done the most good in the world have been those that have been purely and simply declarations of saving truth. It is the exposition of the Word of God which makes most for the moral and spiritual improvement of men. The Word is "the Sword of the Spirit," and surely the Holy Spirit prefers His own Sword to any instrument of our devising.

A sermon need not be limited to the exposition and enforcement of Scripture, for much of helpfulness is to be drawn from the books of nature and of human life. Jesus, in His preaching, opened up many of His texts with illustrations from nature and life. On the other hand, it is remarkable of the sermons of the New Testament that they are expository in nature and that much of the illustrative material used is drawn from incidents in the Old Testament.

There are no better sermon illustrations than those to be found in the Bible itself. This work is intended to aid the preacher and Bible teacher in locating the best of these, for whatever topic he may seek to illumine.

Keith L. Brooke

Sermon Illustrations of the Bible

Topically Arranged

Accountability to God. Dan. 5. Greatest of men will have to acknowledge their accountability to Him. Will be made to know that God rules.

Adversity—Benefits of. 2 Chron. 33: 9-20. In prosperity men forget God, but in adversity they can find no other refuge. Blessed the affliction that brings one to his knees before the throne.

Adversity—Testing. Gen. 39. Loyalty to God brings Joseph into serious testings. God's grace enables him to overcome enemy's assaults. Though world strips us of our possessions, we need not be stripped of virtue.

Affliction—Blessing of. Jn. 4:46-54. Blessed are the trials that drive us to the Lord. The sickness of a son blesses a home.

Affliction—Purpose in. Gen. 44. In times of testing when believers think themselves wronged by men, may learn that God has a righteous purpose—possibly to bring out confession of sin (v. 16).

Afflictions—for God's glory. Jn. 9: 1-41. Is it worth while to go through life blind for the glory of Christ? Tedious afflictions may be consecrated to Him. Blind man's trial resulted in proving Jesus the Light of the world to many souls.

Allegiance to Christ. Ruth 1. Ruth declaring allegiance to Naomi. Many come short of salvation through Christ because they cannot bear to forsake things of Moab and attach themselves to Him. If we let nothing separate us from our duty to Christ, He will let nothing cut off our happiness in Him.

Allegiance to Christ. Ruth. 2. (See v. 22-23.) Ruth's allegiance to Boaz, his fields and servants. If Christ has dealt bountifully with us, let us not be found in other fields seeking happiness and satisfaction of the world.

Alliances—Ungodly. 2 Chron. 18. Some men's kindnesses are dangerous and their society infectious. Can't

hold familiar converse with wicked
men and get no hurt by them.

Anti-Christ. 2 Sam. 17. **Absalom a
type of.** Gathers army against Christ,
the greater David (Rev. 19:19), meeting his defeat in the brightness of
Christ's coming. See ch. 18.

Apostasy. Judges 17. Micah gives
striking illustration of all apostasy.
Had departed entirely from God's revealed will concerning worship and
priesthood, yet exalts a false priesthood.
Expects God's blessing because he has
linked his idolatry to the ancient Le-
vitical order.

Apostasy—The leaven of. Mt. 13:
33-35. Leaven type of evil. True doctrine given for nourishment of children
of the kingdom (Mt. 4:4; 1 Tim. 4:6; 1
Pet. 2:2), will be mingled with corrupt
false doctrine by apostate teachers (1
Tim. 4:1-3; 2 Tim. 2:17, 18; 4:3, 4; 2
Pet. 2:1-3). See use of word leaven in
New Testament (1 Cor. 5:6-8; Mt. 16:
12; Mk. 8:15). If leaven is diffusive
power of Christianity, the tares would
be eradicated before end of harvest.
Meal is never used as a type of any-

thing evil. (See sweet savor offering, Lev. 2:1-3.)

Appreciation for kindness. 2 Kgs. 4:1-17. One way the man of God can show appreciation, by ascertaining the deepest needs of those who have ministered to him and praying God for them.

Assurance of salvation. Gen. 9:13-16. Bow seen on clouds of judgment against sin speaks of cross of Christ where judgment has been visited. Never to be repeated. The believer looks on cross, knows penalty of his sins will not be visited upon him. "It is finished."

Atonement. Gen. 6. Atonement of Christ keeps out waters of judgment and makes believer's position in Christ safe.

Atonement. Illustrated in the Passover. Ex. 12. The believer's deliverance based upon the shedding of the blood of a divinely appointed substitute. Jesus, the perfect Lamb of God (1 Pet. 1:19), was sacrificed on the 14th Nisan. His blood must be applied by faith to the heart. If death

has taken place for us, it cannot come
to us.

Atonement—Isaac a type of. Gen.
22. Isaac, obedient unto death. Abraham spared not his own son, but delivered him up. Ram, type of substi-
tution. Resurrection. See Heb. 11:
17-19.

Atonement. Lev. 16. High priest
entering the holiest pictures Christ entering heaven itself with His own blood
for us (Heb. 9:11, 12). His blood makes
God's throne our mercy seat when otherwise it would have remained a throne
of judgment. Note that for us there
is a rent veil (Mt. 27:51; Heb. 10:19,
20), so we can enter for ourselves into
His presence through Christ.

Backsliders. Lk. 15:3-10. God has a
particular care over backsliding children and follows them with the calls of
His Word and the strivings of the Holy
Spirit until they are found and brought
back.

Backsliders — Restoration for. Jn.
21:15-19. Peter, who had thrice denied
his Lord, is given three opportunities

to reassert his love. Active soul-winning work as a guard against sinning.

Backsliders—Restoration of (Peter). Christ's intercession (Lk. 22:31, 32). Look of Christ (Lk. 22:61). Message of Christ (Mk. 16:7). Interview with Christ (Lk. 24:34). Open confession (Jn. 21:15-17). Restored to his work (Jn. 21:15-17). Back to the starting point (Jn. 21:18, 19—Follow me).

Backsliders—Restoring. Gen. 14. Abram not indifferent to Lot, who had taken way of his own devising. Goes to his aid in spite of past treatment.

Backsliders—The call to. Gen. 35:1. God ever called His wandering child back to Himself. Review Jacob's self-chosen way and show its consequences.

Backsliding—Cost of. Gen. 29. Jacob not forsaken of God but permitted to reap shame and sorrow of self-chosen way.

Backsliding. Gen. 13. Lot gets his eyes on material wealth, loses fellowship with Abram, brings trouble upon himself and family.

Backsliding—Steps in. Mt. 26. Boastfulness (v. 33-35). Unwatchfulness (v. 40). Prayerlessness (v. 41, 45). Fleshly service (v. 51; Jn. 18: 10). Following afar off (v. 58). Fellowship with enemies (v. 69; Lk. 22: 54). Open denial (v. 70-75).

Backsliding—The cost of. Lk. 15: 11-32. God has to bankrupt us when we wander from Him, in order to bring us back to Himself. Many Christians for a time feed on swine's food, but cannot be satisfied by it.

Bereavement—a means of bringing one to know God and His Word. 1 Kgs. 17:17-24. God's power revealed.

Bereavement—Jesus our comfort in. Lk. 7:12-18. May get a blessing if we meet Jesus on the road. He meets us in our saddest journeys and brings us hope. Do not let sorrow unfit for service (v. 13).

Bible—An unread. 2 Kgs. 22-23. An unread Bible is a lost Bible, and a lost Bible means spiritual degeneracy and accompanying curses. When one finds his lost Bible it is quick to find him. Sin keeps one from the Bible or the Bible keeps one from sin.

Bible Study. Josh. 1. Joshua, one of the busiest men, told to meditate on it and talk it (v. 8). True courage comes from being linked up to God's Word and obeying it. Bible verses saved Joshua from reverses.

Blessing—of God. Gen. 48. Jacob blesses contrary to Joseph's wish. God in His grace does not always observe order of nature in bestowing His blessings, nor prefer those we think fittest. Chooses weak to confound mighty.

Blessing—Remembering. 2 Chron. 20:26. Valley of Berachah, lit. "Blessing." (Modern Bible class name "Baraca" taken from this.) Was perpetuated for encouragement of others to trust God and to remind us that our praises should be as oft repeated as our prayers.

Blessings after times of stress. 1 Kgs. 18:42-46. Little cloud size of a man's hand. Great blessings may arise from small beginnings.

Blessings—Spiritual and temporal. Josh. 15:19. Blessings of upper springs illustrate those which relate to our souls, and those of the nether springs speak of those which relate to the body and the life which now is.

Character—Shown in our choices. 2

Chron. 1. Christian's real character appears in his choices. "What wilt thou have?" tries a man as much as "What wouldst thou do?"

Character—Transformation of. Gen. 49. Jacob's life, ending in serenity and blessing, shows God's power to transform character. Trace steps in his experience. His first faith (Gen. 25:28-34). His vision (Gen. 28). His wandering (Gen. 29-31). His transforming experience (Gen. 32). Return to Bethel (Gen. 35). His final walk of faith.

Cheerfulness—Duty of. Acts 23:11. It is Christ's will that we should suffer with Him, but in the trials He would have us be cheerful.

Children—Ability for service. Jn. 6:9. An unnoticed lad played a big part because he became a partner with Jesus.

Children—Born in answer to prayer. 1 Sam. 1. Hannah a rebuke to parents who have no thought of God's glory in connection with bringing children into the world. The child who is dedicated to the Lord (v. 28) will usually be called by the Lord.

Children—Dedicating unborn. Judges 13. Manoah and wife devoting Samson to God before his birth.

Children—Influenced by parents. 2 Kgs. 2:23. These children had been drinking in their parents' discussions of unbelief, and now join their parents in infidelity. Generation of scoffers produced (see 2 Pet. 3:3, 4).

Children. Model boyhood of Jesus. Lk. 2:41-52. Constant growth, physical, intellectual, spiritual (v. 40, 52), filled with wisdom, crowned with grace (v. 40), loved house of God (43, 46, 49), pondered the Word (47), conscious of divine fatherhood (49), obedient to human fatherhood, faithful in present work (51), fitting for larger work (v. 52).

Children—Necessity of restraining. 1 Sam. 2-3. Eli's life work wrecked because of failure to properly restrain evil sons (3:13). Eli like many preachers—too busy with sermons and meetings to look after own sons.

Christ—Authority of. Mk. 9:7. God's voice says listen to Christ's voice.

Christ—Bread of God. Ex. 25 (Shewbread). The shewbread speaks of the life-sustaining Christ. He is the "corn of wheat" (Jn. 12:24) ground in the mill of suffering (Jn. 12:27) and brought into the fire of judgment (Jn. 12:31-33). We feed on Him as having undergone that in our stead and for our sakes.

Christ—Captain of our Salvation. Joshua a type of. Josh. 1, etc. Heb. 2: 10, 11. Comes after Moses (Jn. 1:17). Leads to victory (Rom. 8:37). Our advocate when we have met defeat (1 Jn. 2:1). Allots our portions (Eph. 1: 11, 14).

Christ—Companionship of. Mk. 6: 45-52. Though unseen, He is by our side. Comes to us sometimes in ways we do not recognize Him. If at sea, remember He is ever ready to come to your relief.

Christ—David a type of. 1 Sam. 16. David means "beloved"—type of "the beloved Son " Called from place of obscurity and contempt. So Christ came from humble walk. First anointed by God and later by the people. Christ anointed at His baptism, and at His second coming it will be ratified by His brethren and by all nations.

Christ—Deity of—proven by demons.
Mk. 5:1-20. Demons believe in His deity and tremble before Him. Know that by His word they will ultimately be sent to chains of eternal darkness.

Christ—His covenant with the Father.
1 Sam. 20. Covenant of Jonathan and David illustrates that between God and the Son on behalf of believers. Jn. 10: 28; Rom. 8:32-39.

Christ—His manner of coming to the throne. 2 Sam. 4 (see v. 9). God had hitherto helped David in his difficulties, and in coming to the throne David would depend upon Him and not the devices of men to complete God's purpose. Jesus is coming to the throne not by devices of men to "bring in the kingdom" but by the hand of God Himself.

Christ—His reception as King. 2 Sam. 5. David recognized as king on three counts. Of their flesh (v. 1). Christ, Matt. 25:40. Their leader in battle (v. 2). Christ, Josh. 5:13-15. Designed by God (v. 2). Christ, Rom. 3:25.

Christ—His saving program. Jn. 13: 3, 4, 5, 12, 16. "Arose" from His place in glory, "laid aside garments" of majesty (Phil. 2:6, 7). Took form of a "servant" (Phil. 2:7). Provides "cleansing" (Jn. 15:3). Applies the cleansing water (Eph. 5:26). "Took his garments" again (Jn. 17:5) and is "seated" (Heb. 10:12).

Christ—His triumph over Satan. 1 Sam. 17. David's victory over Goliath, type of triumph of Christ over Satan.

Christ in humiliation. Ex. 16. Bread of life "come down from heaven." A "small thing" (v. 14). Typifies Christ in humiliation, "having no form nor comeliness." As such He must be received by faith. To think on Christ as He went about doing the Father's will is to feed on the manna.

Christ in resurrection, typified by Joseph. Gen. 39-41. The one taken from pit into which he came through rejection by his own. He is coming to the place of ruler and will be channel of blessing to Gentiles.

Christ—Intercession of. Ex. 31-32. Moses as a prince who had power with God illustrated the work of Christ as Intercessor whom the Father heareth always. Through His intercession we obtain constant assurance of the blessings of salvation.

Christ—Isaac type of. Gen. 21. Name given before birth, birth predicted and supernatural. His offering by his father, voluntary. His deliverance from death, type of resurrection. Marriage—bride selected by father. The servant (Holy Spirit) calls the bride. The meeting of the son and his bride.

Christ—Kinsman Redeemer. Boaz, Ruth 3, a type of. Through His incarnation Christ became kin to us as a human being, that we through the Spirit, might become betrothed to Him. By sin, we had forfeited our inheritance. Christ, the only one who can take up the documents and restore us to position.

Christ—Love of. 1 Sam. 18. Jonathan's love illustrates the love of Christ for us. He stripped Himself to clothe us (Phil. 2:5-7).

Christ—made sin for us. Brazen serpent a type of. Num. 21; 2 Cor. 5: 21. Serpent a symbol of sin judged. Brass, type of divine judgment. Hence brazen serpent speaks of Christ bearing our judgment. See Jn. 3:14, 15. The race perishing in sin (Rom. 3:10-12). Christ the divinely appointed cure. Cured by a look (Jn. 1:29). Sting of sin incurable by human means.

Christ—Moses a type of. Ex. 2, etc. As prophet (Acts 3:22-23). Advocate (Ex. 32:31-35; 1 Jn. 2:1, 2). Intercessor (Ex. 17:1-6; Heb. 7:25). Leader (Deut. 33:4, 5; Heb. 2:10).

Christ—Moses a type of. Ex. 2, etc. Rejected by Israel, he turns to Gentiles. In his rejection takes Gentile bride, then later appears as Israel's deliverer and is accepted.

Christ our example. Ex. 12:8. Christ can not be our example until He is our atoning sacrifice. The lamb must be "roast with fire" (not raw). Speaks of Christ subjected to fires of God's wrath against sin. Christ cannot be feasted on unless He is accepted as the sin-bearer. Secured by His atoning work, we may feast on Him in peace.

Christ—our High Priest. Ex. 28. Our great high priest bears the names of His own on His breast before God, presenting them as those "accepted in the beloved."

Christ—our Intercessor. Deut. 10: 10, 11. Moses, intercessor and commander of Israel, type of Christ who ever lives to make intercession for His own, who has all power in heaven and earth to give us victory and who leads us by His Spirit.

Christ—our light. Ex. 25 (v. 31). Candlestick type of Christ shining in the fulness of the power of the seven-fold Spirit (Heb. 1:9; Rev. 1:4). Natural light excluded from the tabernacle. Must put out our own lights if we would have light of Christ.

Christ—our Mediator. Deut. 5:1-5. Moses stood between—type of Christ who stands between God and man as the true Mediator so we may hear from God and speak to Him without fear of the fires of His holiness.

Christ—our Peace. Lev. 3. Peace offering fulfilled in Christ who "made peace" (Col. 1:20), proclaimed peace (Eph. 2:17), and is our peace (Eph. 2: 14). In Him God and a sinner can meet in peace. God is propitiated, the sinner reconciled. Note that this is at cost of blood and fire.

Christ—"our Passover." Ex. 12. Israelites, in offering lamb, recognized

their inability to save themselves and
necessity of placing another between
them and consequences of sin. Christ
"the Lamb of God."

**Christ, our Provider. Elijah a type
of.** 1 Kgs. 17. Cf. v. 13, "Bring it to
me," with Mt. 14:18.

Christ, our Refuge. Num. 35. Cities
of refuge type of Christ, sheltering the
sinner from judgment (Rom. 8:33, 34;
Phil. 3:9; Heb. 6:18, 19).

Christ our Sacrifice. Lev. 1. Burnt
offering speaks of Christ who offered
Himself without spot to God in de-
light to do the Father's will even unto
death. Fire symbol of God's holiness,
which consumed the offering. Laying
on of the offerer's hand (v. 4) was to
show he was identifying himself with
the offering—speaking of believer's
faith in accepting and identifying himself with Christ (Rom. 4:5; 6:3-11).

Christ our Scapegoat. Lev. 16:11.
One goat slain as token of satisfaction
to God's justice. Other sent away as
token of sin actually dismissed from
sinner. Wilderness symbol of abode
of evil things (Is. 13:21; 34:14).

Christ — the Shepherd King. 1 Chron. 17:7-8. David here a type of the Son of God after the flesh (Mt. 1: 1; Rom. 1:3)—the shepherd king. In His first coming He took the shepherd's place in death (Jn. 10:11), now in resurrection power (Heb. 13:20).

Christ—our Sin Bearer. Lev. 4. The sin offering shows Christ laden with the believer's sins, standing in the sinner's stead (cf. Is. 53; 2 Cor. 5:21).

Christ—our Source of life. Jn. 15. Vine and branches. We are branches in true vine from which we draw hourly the divine life. Draw all wisdom and strength from Him.

Christ—our Substitute. Lev. 17:11. Explains the meaning of the sacrifices. Every offering expressed the sentence of law upon a substitute for the offender, pointing toward substitutional death of Christ, which alone vindicated the righteousness of God (Rom. 3:24, 25).

Christ—our Wilderness Bread. Ex. 16. Jesus the Bread of life is ministered to us through the Word, by the Spirit. He can be partaken of unre-

servedly, but we have no more of Him
than faith appropriates (v. 16).

Christ—Power of. Mt. 9. Has all
power in heaven and earth. Degradation and disease (v. 20), demons (v.
33), death (v. 25), are subject to His
rebuke. Faith in Him, the most price-
less treasure on earth (vs. 2, 22, 29).

Christ—Prince of Peace. 1 Chron.
29: 23-25. Solomon's glorious and
peaceful kingdom a type of the coming
millennial kingdom. His will indeed
be "the throne of the Lord" (v. 23).

**Christ, Prince of Peace. Solomon a
type of.** 1 Kgs. 1:39, 40. (See Is. 9:
6; 1 Chron. 22:9.) Jesus does not fulfill
the Solomon type until after He has
fulfilled the David type. Chosen before born (Is. 42:1). Rode into Jerusalem on a mule (Jn. 12:14-16). A-
nointed (Acts 10:38). Peace will fill
the earth when His reign is set up
(Zech. 14:9).

Christ—Reign of, delayed. 1 Sam.
26 (v. 24). David's way to throne lay
through multiplied difficulties. Christ,
though anointed King with undisputed
title, yet remains meek and lowly,

awaiting the set time for His actual
reign over all.

Christ—Resurrection of. Jonah (Mt.
12:40) type of Christ who was buried
and arose (1 Cor. 15:4), after three
days. Both were buried in order to
their rising again for the bringing of
the doctrine of repentance to the Gentile world.

Christ—Resurrection of. Num. 17.
Illustrated in Aaron's rod that budded.
Christ in His resurrection was owned
of God as High Priest. All authors of
religion have died, but Christ alone
was raised from the dead to be a high
priest (Heb. 4:14; 5:4-10). Resurrection proves Christ the chosen one (Rom.
1:4).

Christ—Satanic opposition to. Mk.
14:32-35. What "hour" and "cup"
was Jesus seeking to be delivered from?
Does He pray for deliverance from the
cross—the very purpose for which He
had come into the world? (Jn. 12:27).
Heb. 5:7 shows His prayer was heard
and answered. See Lk. 22:44; Mk. 14:
34. Shows Satan was attempting to
kill Him before He could accomplish
His purpose in the appointed way. Lk.

22:43 is the answer to His prayer. He was saved from death in Gethsemane. When hour of the cross comes, He asks for no angels or defenders and rebukes Peter for trying to defeat God's plan (Mt. 26:52, 53, 56).

Christ—Saul a picture of. 1 Sam. Saul raised up to save Israel. Anointed —Acts 10:38. Although anointed, acted as servant of father, Jn. 6:38. Touched with compassion for people, Mt. 9:36. Spirit came upon him, Mt. 3:16. Became salvation of his followers, 1 Pet. 3:18. Full of grace to those who had rebelled against him, Jn. 1:17. Went down to Gilgal a second time. Was openly declared king, Rev. 19:11-16.

Christ—Sovereign over every ailment. Mt. 8. Over physical ailments (v. 2, 6, 14), emissaries of Satan and over sin (v. 16; Mt. 9:5). Faith takes Him at His word and finds rest and deliverance.

Christ, the solver of problems. Joseph a type, Gen. 41, of Christ, the one who is able to solve all our vexing problems and relieve our hearts of all burdens.

Christ—The resurrected. Josh. 3-4. Christ, our Joshua, went through the Jordan of death, opening the way for all who would believe, to follow Him. Appointed twelve apostles (according to the tribes of Israel) by the memorial of the Gospel, to transmit the knowledge of this to remote places and future ages.

Christ—the Resurrection and Life. Jn. 11. He is the fountain of life and the head and the author of physical resurrection.

Christ—the Rock. Ex. 17:5-7 (cf. 1 Cor. 10: 4). He is the smitten rock out of which comes the "water of life"—the Holy Spirit's saving power. Until the rock was smitten, the streams of salvation were pent up.

Christ, the True Temple. 1 Kgs. 5. Illustrated in Solomon's temple. See Jn. 2:21. God Himself prepared Him (Eph. 1:4; Heb. 10:5). In Him all God's spiritual children meet and through Him have access to God.

Christ, the Wisdom of God. Solomon a type of. 1 Kgs. 3 and 4. Christ in whom are hidden all the treasures of wisdom and knowledge—hidden for a use—that he might be "made unto us wisdom."

Christ—Typified in Joseph. Gen. 37. Joseph the beloved of his father, hated by brethren, his claims rejected, conspired against, in intent and figure was slain, in resurrection gains Gentile bride, eventually reconciled to his brethren, who are exalted with him.

Christian Science. Inverts the divine order. Mk. 2:14, 15. Preaching the Gospel precedes the healing of the body.

Christian Science. Job 2:5. The foundation stone of this cult. Body healing is exalted above healing of the soul. Men will embrace anything that will relieve pain of body. Satan uses physical ailments to draw men from God.

Christians—Temple a type of. 1 Kgs. 6-7. Believers are habitations of God (1 Cor. 3:16, 17; 6:19). Should be as beautiful a temple as the Holy Spirit, the Builder, can make it. Yield to His Master strokes.

Church—as bride of Christ. Isaac securing his bride (Gen. 24). Abraham type of the Father (Mt. 22:2). Serv-

ant type of Holy Spirit who calls the
bride (Jn. 16:13, 14). Servant type of
Spirit enriching the bride (1 Cor. 12:
7-11). Rebekah type of church, the
"called out" virgin bride (2 Cor. 11:
2; Eph. 5:25-32). Isaac type of Bride-
groom going out to receive His bride
(1 Thess. 4:14-16).

Church—Bride of Christ. Song Sol.
The spiritual interpretation of the book
is of Christ the Son and His heavenly
bride (2 Cor. 11:1-4). The church is
beautiful to Christ as Christ is beautiful to the church.

Church—Differences in. Acts 15.
When serious differences in regard to
God's Word arise, let men of God come
together for prayer and mutual advice.

**Church—Necessity of the Holy Spirit
in.** 1 Kgs. 8. All cost and pains are
lost on stately structures unless God
has been in the work. If He fails to
manifest His glory in them they are but
ruinous heaps.

Church—Purchased by Christ. Mt.
13:45-46. Church the pearl of great
cost. Pearl is one, a perfect symbol
of unity (1 Cor. 10:17; 12:12, 13; Eph.
4:4-6). Formed by accretion, and that

not mechanically but vitally, as Christ adds to the church (Acts 2:41, 47; 5: 14; 11:24; Eph. 2:21; Col. 2:19). Christ, having given Himself for the pearl, now prepares it for presentation to Himself (Eph. 5:25-27).

Church, the Gentile bride. Typified by Asenath (Gen. 41:45-57), the Gentile bride espoused to Joseph, the rejected one. She is type of church, called out from Gentiles.

Church—The ideal congregation in. Acts 10:33. Good recipe for all who listen to sermons. Ideal congregation is unanimous, devout and eager.

Church—The ministries of. Acts 6. Those called to preach the Word must not neglect the special ministry for church activities that should be carried on by others. Those engaged in any part of the church work, regardless of how menial the task, need to be free from scandal, possessed of discretion and filled with the Spirit.

Church—The true (completion of). Illustrated by building of tabernacle (Ex. 36). Souls redeemed by Christ are the materials from which the Gospel tabernacle is being built (1 Pet. 2:5).

Those called to the building of this house are those whom God has made fit for the work. Have ability and willingness.

✠ **Church—The True.** Gen. 2:18-25, Eve a type. A bride needful to Adam, as church needful to Christ. Born out of opened side of the man—church out of the pierced side of Christ. Eve nearest to Adam as church is to Christ. Adam's deep sleep—Christ's three days' sleep before church born. "Bone of my bone"—as church is member of Christ's body, flesh and bones—one spirit with Him.

Church—True. Formation of. Lev. 23:15-22. Illustrated in feast of Pentecost. Speaks of descent of Holy Spirit to form church. Leaven is present, for the church is not perfect (Mt. 13:33; Acts 5:1, 10; 15:1). Note in this feast there are "loaves," not separate "sheaves." Real union of particles, making a homogeneous body (1 Cor. 10:16, 17; 12:12, 13, 20).

Church—True. Gen. 13:14-18; 15:3-6. Abram's earthly and spiritual seed. Dust of earth—Abram's earthly seed, the Jews. Stars of heaven, Ab-

ram's spiritual seed, the true church,
the heavenly people.

Church—Typified in Ruth. Book of
Ruth as a foreview of church (Ruth the
Gentile bride), Christ (the Bethlehem-
ite who is able to redeem).

Church—Unity in. Acts 2. The condition of spiritual blessing. Cannot
breathe power of the Spirit upon a dis-
cordant church. Be united, expectant,
prayerful, and His power will come and
fill the church.

**Church—Work of—done decently
and quietly.** Illustrated in building of
the temple (1 Kgs. 6). Noise and no-
toriety not marks of spiritual progress
(1:7). In building the spiritual temple, quietness and order become and
befriend the work.

Circumstances — Deliverance from.
Ex. 14:13, 15. God, by the shed blood,
comes between us and the enemy of
our souls. By His presence, if we look
to Him, He is ready to come between
us and every overcoming circumstance.
When outlook is bad, take the uplook.

Common Tasks—Acts 9:36-43. No
matter how mean the calling, the Holy
Spirit can make it great. Dorcas as

truly a missionary as one who goes out
to preach.

Communion with Jesus. Lk. 24:13-
35. We draw Him to our side by having an honest desire for truth (v. 15).
Possible to talk about Him yet not
really know Him (v. 16). His presence enjoyed makes the days seem short
(v. 27, 28).

Common Tasks—Influence of. 1
Sam. 20:36-38. Lad who ran after ar-
rows was unconsciously bearing tidings
of great import. As we work, our lives
may speak for life or for condemnation.

Common Tasks. Lk. 2:41-52. Ten-
elevenths of Jesus' life lived at Naz-
areth—quiet humdrum life. Glorified
God in the common tasks until it was
God's will for Him to undertake larger
things.

Communion with Christ. Acts 27:
21-25. The secret of abiding peace and
abounding service in the midst of greatest storms of life.

Communion with Christ. Lev. 23:
6-8. Feast of unleavened bread speaks
of Christ the unleavened (sinless)
Bread of God and of the necessity of
our holiness in order to fellowship with

Him. Note the divine order—the redemption feast has to precede this (v. 4, 5). We must first be redeemed before we can feed on Christ.

Communion with Christ. Lk. 10:38-42. Essential to highest service for Christ. Our love to Him becomes alloyed with selfish pride unless we take time to sit at His feet.

Communion with Christ. Mt. 17. Jesus does not go where His disciples may not come. Only three of the twelve enjoyed the mountain-top experience. He is transfigured to His own in the ratio of three to twelve. How few George Mullers, Andrew Murrays, etc. Such visions of Him calculated to remove all doubts as to His divine sonship and purpose in going to the cross, as well as surety of His glorious return.

Communion with God. Gen. 35. Jacob comes back to Bethel (house of God). Imperfect communion with God until all idols are put out and we come into His presence as He directs.

Communion with God. 1 Sam. 3. Danger of mistaking God's voice for man's and man's voice for God's. Needs childlike, purged heart to distinguish.

Craftiness of world. Ex. 1:10. Wise dealing of enemies of God's people is folly, for God says they "shall be as sand of sea."

Compassion—God's, for lost sinners. 2 Sam. 14. David's compassion as a father prevails to reconcile him to an impenitent son. See v. 33. Can penitent sinners doubt the compassion of God, in His Son, when they truly come to Him?

Complaining against God. Ex. 5:15-23. God sometimes employs strange methods when coming toward His people in mercy. They in their unbelief, think themselves ill-treated. By trials God seeks to cause us to cease from man and from depending on second causes.

Complaining against God. Job 2. If trial makes us complain against God, the devil laughs and is glad. Meant to be an evidence of God's love to those who love Him, for to such He gives abundant supplies of grace to bear it and glorify Him.

Complaining. Num. 11. Kadesh-Barnea e x p e r i e n c e. Unconverted church members with no healthy ap-

petite for Bread of God, clamor for
things pleasing to the flesh in the work
and way of the church.

Compromise. Josh. 9. God's people
have often compromised with wily enemies of His cause, simply because they
argued antiquity. Better to consult
God's Word than compromise with any
sect that plays the Gibeonitish strat-
agem.

Compromise—R e f u s i n g. Dan. 3.
Obey the powers that be until they require us to disobey and dishonor God
(Rom. 13:1), then obey God rather than
man (Acts 5:29). If called upon to
pass through fire, Christ will be there
with us. Nothing lost by being true to
Him.

Compromise—Refusing to. 1 Sam.
11. God has given us a leader for every
crisis, so it is not necessary for His
people to compromise with the world,
if they will trust Him. Through Christ
our King we may have the victory.

**Condemning others—The inconsist-
ency of.** Jn. 8:1-11. Easy to condemn
our own sins when seen in others.

Conscience—an insufficient guide.

Acts 9. A conscientious man may be thoroughly wrong. Cf. v. 1 with 26:9.

Consecration. Ex. 28:39-43. Consecration of Aaron and sons, a type of our consecration. Must first belong to priestly family (Rev. 1:8). Properly clothed (Rev. 19:7, 8). Must have the right consecrator (Moses type of Christ as consecrator). Note that Aaron did not consecrate himself, but only presented himself for it (Rom. 12:1). See ch. 29. In Aaron's arms were put the parts of the sacrifice which typify the inherent richness of power of Christ. Waving this before God, they thus acknowledged that the power for service was not in themselves, but in another.

Consecration. Need of giving all we have into His hands by faith. Ex. 10:8-24. Danger of compromise by desiring for our children a position in the world (v. 11) or by failing to consecrate all our possessions along with ourselves.

Consecration of our all. Jn. 12:3. Hair, woman's chief adornment. The highest things of human glory and beauty are lower than the lowest that pertain to God. The greatest marks of beauty are only good when doing service for Him.

Confession of sin. Hard to bring men to it. 1 Sam. 15. Saul and followers try to justify themselves rather than confess wrong. Try to make ceremonial observances take the place of full yieldedness to Christ.

Conquest—Christian. Josh. 10-11. Israel first helped by miracles—but in ch. 11, left to make own efforts. So war carried on against Satan's kingdom in this age was first advanced by miracles, but it being sufficiently proved by them to be of God, we are now left to ordinary help of divine grace in Christ and need not look for standing still of the sun, hailstones, etc.

Consistent life. Sweetness of Naomi's home life the means of drawing Ruth to her and to her God. Ruth 1: 16-19. If there were more older women like Naomi, would be more younger women like Ruth.

Consolation—Human—imperfect and inadequate. Job 4-5. Many in trying to console others only add to their grief because they do not come with a message from God. See 4:14, 15.

Dogmatists who have to be listened to because they have had some ONE remarkable experience and think everyone else's case is like their own. Truest comfort is from God's Word. Rom. 15:4.

Conspiracy—The meanest. 2 Sam. 15. He who steals one heart away from another by means of innuendos is the vilest of robbers, especially when professed devotion to God is used as a pretext to carry out the design (v. 7).

Counselling with the ungodly. 1 Kgs. 12. Rehoboam and the young men. Taking advice from unspiritual men spells blunder. If we make God the source of our counsel (Jas. 3:15) we will avoid all folly. Older men not usually on side of evil. Conflicting counsel of men.

Covetousness—Ahab's. 1 Kgs. 21. One may covet and get what it is not God's will for him to have, and then get a curse along with it. Covetousness opens the door to all sin.

Covetousness—Dangers of. Acts 5. First sin in Eden (Gen. 3:6). First in the promised land (Josh. 7:21). First in the early church. Some are ambitious to be counted liberal while in reality they seek to retain much for self.

Cross—Power of. Ex. 14:19-20. Illustrated by the pillar of cloud to the Israelites. It was the foundation of peace for believers, but sealed the condemnation of the enemies of God.

Death. Ex. 15:23-25. Bitter waters as type of death. The Christ of the "tree" went into the waters that they henceforth should yield only sweetness to the believer.

Delays — God's. Jn. 11. Don't worry about His delays (Is. 54:7, 8). He tarries that greater things may be done for us.

Denying Christ. Mk. 14:53-72. Jesus grieved more by denials of professed friends than by the opposition of avowed enemies. Peter, trusting in his own love to Christ, denied his Lord. Later, trusting in Christ's love to him, he stood. Jn. 13:37.

Despondency. Jn. 20:19-29. Thomas was off looking on the dark side of things. Jesus appeared with a message of peace to those who were holding on in prayer. Isolation is conducive to misery of heart.

Despondency—True Christian beyond. Acts 27:32-36. Nothing can make a trusting Christian blue. Will cheerfully minister to others even in the midst of calamities.

Devotion to Christ. Jn. 20. Mary's devotion to Christ. To stay while others stay is the world's love. To stay alone is divine love. Given to woman to first proclaim the resurrection message.

Devotion to Christ. Mt. 26:6-13. Uncalculating love that does not wait until it is too late, to bestow all we have.

Difficulties—God's removal of. Josh. 3. Believers are to go on in way of duty in spite of obstacles that seem to be impassable. Nothing too hard for Jehovah. Step forward in faith and as we do so, the dark waters part for us.

Difficulties. Num. 13-14. Kadesh-Barnea and report of spies. Unbelief looks at God through difficulties. **Faith** looks at difficulties through God. Christians are ever getting frightened at giants in the land.

Difficulties—Trusting God to solve.
Acts 12. God can bring us a discharge
if we regulate our pace to fall in with
His (v. 9). March right up to the difficulty (v. 10). Nothing can hinder
when God is working out our deliverance.

Discipline of God's people. Num.
15-20. Israel's wandering and the
necessary discipline of the redeemed
people. Red Sea, Marah, Elim, Sinai,
were God's ways in discipline and have
counterpart in Christian experience.

Discouragement—Believer's. 1 Sam.
27. Discouragement besets those who
have been undergoing long trials. No
advantage to cross over into borders of
the world for comfort. Cannot expect
God's protection there when we are out
of His will.

Discouragement. E l i j a h under
juniper tree. 1 Kgs. 19. Even though
we faint in our faith, God abides faithful. When discouraged, best thing is to
go where we can see from God's view-
point (1:11)—by coming before God in
prayer. Get out from under the juniper
tree.

Discouragement—Folly of giving way to. Lk. 5:1-11. Because we have tried and failed is no reason why we should not try again, if Jesus bids us. "Launch out" on His promises and try again.

Discouragements in service. Ex. 18: 18-21. Always someone to tell us we are taking on too much. We are not called to service on the ground of our ability. Note that God ignored Jethro's scheme (Num. 11:14-17) and put in its place His own order.

Doubt—Folly of. Jn. 20:19-29. Unbelief wants to see (v. 25). Faith believes to see and finds peace (Ps. 27: 13). Some claim to be "doubting Thomases" who are not, like Thomas, ready to go all the way to know the truth.

Doubt—Folly of. Mt. 14:31. Folly of taking the eyes off Jesus. Peter in his sinking moment looks unto Jesus' face and cannot say a word for himself in answer to the question, "Wherefore?"

Doubts—How to remove. Lk. 7:19-23. Best place to take doubts is direct to Jesus. His mighty works will drive them away.

Education—not a means of saving souls. Acts 17:15-21. Where great learning flourished idolatry most abounded.

Emotion—Friendly. 1 Sam. 20:41,42. Jonathan and David. Manly emotion.

Enemies—Compassion on. Gen. 42. Joseph the one cruelly treated by his brethren, preserves them when they are in deep trial. The best cure for an enemy.

Enemies—Deliverance from—The joy of. Esther 8:16. The holy joy of those who trust in God is a great ornament to God's people and encourages others to trust Him for deliverance.

Enemies—Fear of. Ezra 3. If we have enemies, safest course is to keep on intimate terms with God through His Son, who is typified in the daily Lamb, and whose righteousness must be our confidence in all our supplications.

Enemies—God's power over. 2 Kgs. 7:6,7. The wicked flee when no man pursues. God can dispirit the boldest enemy of Christ's cause and make stoutest heart to tremble at the shaking of a leaf.

Enemies—Kindness a good weapon against. 1 Sam. 24. David rewards Saul good for evil. If we acknowledge God in our ways, He will baffle designs of enemies for us and turn their counsels in our favor.

Enemies—Misrepresent God's people. Esther 3:8. Enemies would not get far in opposing God's work in the world if they did not first utterly misrepresent, in order to give God's people a bad name.

Enemies—No need of fearing. 2 Sam. 16. See v. 9-10. David here is like Christ, who rebuked His disciples who, in zeal for His honor, would have used their miraculous powers on the heads of those who affronted Him (Lk. 9:55).

Enemies—The confusion of. Acts 23:7-10. God can make conspirators' own tongues betray them and the persecutions of His people to turn to the wider spread of the Gospel.

Enemies—their methods. Acts 26: 24, 25. Some who can't prove Chris-

tianity a bad thing try to make out that
Christians are "cracked," and call
preachers cranks. Christians can rejoice at least that heaven will be their
lunatic asylum.

**Enemies — their methods against
Christianity.** Acts 21:27-40. When
they can't prove Christianity a bad
thing, they set about to give it a bad
name. They suddenly show great
concern for the country's laws.

Enemies—Victory over. 1 Kgs. 20:13,
14. Enemies are more than a match
for us but no match for Jehovah. One
with God is a majority (Rom. 8:31).

Enemies—what to do about them.
Lk. 18:1-8. Pray about them (v. 7)
unceasingly until God works out His
own way with them.

Envy. Gen. 37-47. Joseph envied
by his brothers. Envy hates those
excellencies it cannot reach. Is a
canker to the soul and only stops at
murder.

Envy. 1 Sam. 18:1-9. Sign the Spirit
has departed from a man when he can't
endure to hear others praised. Only
way to keep down weeds of envy is to

think less of reputation and more of duty.

Envy. 1 Sam. 19. Envy allowed its way becomes murderous. Tries to get others to share in its sins. Cut the claws of envy lest it become a full-grown tiger when it is too late.

Estrangement from God. 2 Chron. 28. Generally followed by seeking protection from enemies of God (v. 16). No enemy can ever strengthen the people of God (v. 20). There is such a thing as a fatal help (v. 23).

Exaltation—Human. Naboth's. 1 Kgs. 21:12-16. Elevation at hands of men often proves death trap. If running for office, look out for the design of the gang.

Faith—and resources. Mk. 6:32-44. True faith does not neglect resources within reach of man's toil and study (v. 38). Test of faith is to obey Jesus' orders, no matter how strange.

Faith—Childlike. 2 Kgs. 5. Naaman had to become as a little child before God could help him. When he took child's attitude toward God, he became a child (v. 14). See 1 Pet. 2:2.

Faith—Conquest of. Judges 7. Empty pitchers (v. 16) type of earthly body emptied of self (2 Cor. 4:7) but filled with God's Word, the lamp (Ps. 119:105). Pitcher was not to be spared in the advance and lamp was to be held forth (v.20;Phil. 2:16). With trumpet, tidings of victory were sounded (Mk. 16:15).

Faith—Example of. Mt. 8:5-13. Faith knows God's bonds are as good as ready money. Can believe Christ even at a distance.

Faith. Ex. 14:22,23. Stepping out where one cannot see safety, yet trusting God's promises. Sea opened to them step by step as they went forward.

Faith—Foundation of. Lk. 7:1-10. Natural soil of faith is a loving, humble heart (v. 7). Jesus marvels at such faith (v. 9).

Faith—Made one through. Mk. 7: 24-30. By true faith all distinctions between Jew and Gentile, clean and unclean, are swept away. "All one in Christ Jesus"—through simple contact of faith.

Faith. Mk. 5:25-34. Simple touch of faith connects with omnipotent power of God. Jesus discerns the true touch of faith.

Faith—Power over difficulties. 2 Kgs. 2:14. Smiting the waves of difficulty with Elijah's mantle—faith.

Faith—Preparations of. Have the empty vessels ready and God will fill them according to the capacity we provide for Him. 2 Kgs. 4:1-7. Will do abundantly above all we ask or think.

Faith—Saving. Ex. 12:7. The shedding of the blood of the Lamb of God to redeem us does not save until we have appropriated it to our hearts by faith. Blood had to be struck upon door posts, otherwise was not a protection.

Faith—Saving. Mk. 3:1-5. Man with a withered hand typical of those powerless to work for Christ. "Stand forth"—step out on the promises of Christ's Word. "Stretch forth hand" —the endeavor to obey Christ wins the power to obey.

Faith — Source of. Mt. 14:22-36. No sea too rough on which to venture if eyes are fixed on Christ and He bids us come. Steps of faith fall on a seeming void and always find a rock. Faith is always a venture.

Faith—Takes Jesus at His word Lk. 5. Peter let down net where he had fished all night in vain, and where he couldn't see prospects. May seem foolish at times to obey Jesus, but it pays to obey His word implicitly.

Faith—Taking God at His word. Acts 27:25. Faith founded on God's Word has a sure outlook.

Faith—Great. Lk. 7:9. Little faith will bring the soul to heaven, but great faith brings heaven to the soul.

Faith—Taking Jesus at His word. Jn. 4:46-54. The man believed Jesus and counted the transaction done (v. 50) even before he had gone home. Faith sees with God's eye.

Faith—Tests of. Mk. 4:35-41. Jesus had been teaching disciples all day—now tests their faith to see what they have learned. Said, "Let us pass over," —should have assured them of arrival. When storm arises they are faithless and rebuke Him. If He was at perfect rest, could there have been real

danger of their perishing? See v. 40.
God's storm can only help God's business—why the faithless with Jesus on
board?

Faith—Trials of. 1 Sam. 14:4. Faith
of Jonathan is proved by encountering
sharp rocks. Nevertheless he counts
on God (v. 6) and pushes ahead. Rom.
8:31.

Faith—Vicarious. Lk. 7:1-10. Power
of faith exercised for others, who may
be at a great distance away.

Faith—Victory of. Josh. 6. Fall of
Jericho accomplished by means and
upon principles utterly foolish and inadequate in the view of human wisdom (1 Cor. 1:17-29). If faith is absolutely obedient to divine precepts,
it can remove mountains.

Faith—Wonders of. 2 Kgs. 7:1,2.
Faith expects from God what is beyond all human expectation. Those
who cannot take God at His word forfeit the benefit of His promises.

Faithfulness—Reward of. Gen. 41.
Joseph the faithful believer is abundantly recompensed for the disgrace he
patiently suffers. His exaltation gives

him opportunity to let many know the power of God.

Faithfulness—to small tasks. Jonathan's armor-bearer. 1 Sam. 14. Faithful to his opportunity as armor-bearer, an important cog in the plan of God.

False cause—Support of a. Acts 24. Every false cause can find men of sharp wits to plead it. If God's people can answer with the language of a clear conscience, they have nothing to fear.

False Teachings. 1 Kgs. 12:25-33. Golden calf set up where first altar to God had stood (v. 29. See Gen. 12:8). All isms originate in man's heart (v. 26), have a selfish purpose back of them (v. 27-29) and are launched on a pretense that it is for the people's good. Always tend to sin and idolatry.

Fame—True. 1 Kgs. 10. Solomon's fame draws attention to his God, the source of his knowledge. True fame has name of the Lord associated with it and challenges inquiry into the means of God's grace.

Family. Denying Satan. A hold on any member of. Ex. 10:8-23. Moses would not compromise by leaving any of the little ones behind. Many godly parents desire worldly prosperity and position for their children.

Faults—Our own. 2 Kgs. 11:13-16. Athaliah, the embodiment of treason, cries treason at others. Men detest their own faults when they see them in others.

Fear—Expression of doubt. Gen. 33. Jacob fears Esau. Had he believed God's promise concerning himself, would not have anticipated destruction. Fear is ingenious. If we have power with God, will have power with man.

Fear—The unbeliever's. 1 Sam. 18:12, 29. When Saul was in Satan's power he was always a prey to fear. (Ps. 53:5; 2 Tim. 1:7; Ps. 46:1-3).

Fear—Result of evil. 2 Kgs. 6 (see v. 11). The wicked have heart trouble (Is. 67:20). Only cure for heart trouble —Jn. 14:1.

Fidelity to God. Dan. 6. God first is safety first. God knows the heart, and whatever the test, will give peace and deliverance, and will clear the integrity of His trusting child.

Food—Spiritual. Ex. 16. Believer must gather fresh spiritual food every day, letting the Holy Spirit minister it to our hearts (v. 19). Spiritual food cannot be hoarded. Must feed on Christ for daily needs. Cannot be sustained on past appropriations of Christ.

Forbearance—Parental. 2 Sam. 18. How bad a child may be to the best of fathers and how good a father may be to the worst of children. How a father sometimes, out of love for a son, will overlook the best interests of those about him.

Forgetfulness of Christ's favors. Mk. 8:14-21. Christ is provoked when we are overwhelmed with present distress, because we so soon forget what we have seen of His goodness, in supplying our needs in days past.

Forgiveness—Law of. Mt. 18:21-35. God is pleased with those who multiply their pardons of others, even as they have many times been pardoned by Him.

Forgiveness. Lev. 16:11. Illustrated in the scapegoat. When our sins are pronounced upon Christ our Scapegoat, they are carried away into oblivion, never to appear against us again. "As far as east is from west." (See v. 22.) The land of forgetfulness (Is. 43:25).

Formalism—Dead. Lk. 10:31. Some wear the livery of the church whose religion is a routine of dead things. They open with hireling hand the temple gates.

Formalism. Mk. 3 (v. 2). To formalists a breach of external piety is more shocking than a breach of principle. Who most honored the Sabbath—the plotters or the One who healed?

Friendship. Jonathan and David. 1 Sam. 20. True friendship translates itself into deeds (v. 5). Absolutely frank (v. 9). Warns of danger (v. 9). Devoted (v. 41-42).

Fruit-bearing. Jn. 15. When Christ has to purge the branches, it is not a proof of worthlessness, but of the possibility of fruit, and the pledge of more. Can't depend on own power for fruits of the Spirit. Will be laid aside if we refuse to draw our life from Him.

Fruitlessness. Mt. 21:18-21. Leaves a type of Christian testimony. Tree

with leaves but no fruit picture of
Christian who professes but bears no
fruit. Many Christians become withered because of persistent rebellion
against the will of God.

Giving. 2 Kgs. 12. Would be plenty
in Lord's treasury if people gave with
both heart and hand (v. 4, 10). If no
sacrifice in giving, no blessing.

Giving—How God regards our. Lk.
21:1-4. Jesus watching rich men and
judging them by what they keep to
themselves. Widow had little of it, but
there was much in it.

Giving what we have. Jn. 6:1-13.
The little we have, if put in Jesus' hands
will be multiplied many times. See v.
9. Selfishness with much can do little.
Love with a little can do much.

God—Folly of resisting. Ex. 8. God
can make all His creatures to be at war
with us. Can arm smallest parts of His
creation against men. He often chooses
contemptible instruments to defeat
those who are against Him.

God—Greatness and humility of. Ex.
21. The great God of heaven stoops to
take interest in the detail affairs be-

tween man and man. Regulates even to
the loss of a tooth.

God—Immutability of. Ex. 3:13, 14.
Same yesterday, today and forever.

God—Presence of. Ex. 3. Fire a
frequent emblem of God (Ex. 13:21;
19:18; 24:17; Deut. 4:24; Ps. 97:3;
Acts 2:3) and appears as accompani-
ment and indication of His presence.
Burning bush pictures God humbling
Himself to manifest His presence in a
little thorn bush. Speaks of His un-
diminished yet unreplenished energy,
and of His consuming and purifying
holiness.

Good deeds—Eternity of. Mk. 14:1-9.
No good action or example can die. The
deed leaves an indelible stamp on time.

Gospel—Objectors to. Acts 19:23-41.
Some oppose the Gospel because it
would call them off from their sinful
employments. Many churches have a
Demetrius who gets suddenly religious
when anything comes up that affects his
trade.

Grace—Sarah a type of. Grace as the
"free woman." See Gal. 4:22-31.

Grace—Streams of. Num. 20. The

abundant water coming from the smitten rock (see Ex. 17:5), tells of refreshing streams of grace reaching the need of the people in spite of the errors of their leaders (v. 10). See 1 Cor. 10:4.

Grace—Wonders of God's. 2 Kgs. 6. The God of nature not tied up to laws of nature as we understand them. As He raised iron against natural laws, so His grace can raise the iron heart which has sunk into mud of this world and raise up affections naturally earthly, to things above.

Grafters. Gehazi, the first. 2 Kgs. 5:20-27. Got what he wanted and leprosy along with it.

Greatness—True. Gen. 47. Joseph exalting those who have mistreated him. Measure of truly great man is way he treats men who have been small toward him.

Grief over death of loved ones. Jn. 11. Profound belief in the words of Jesus will prove the balm for stricken hearts.

Guidance of the Holy Spirit. Acts 21. Disregard of any of the details of the leading of the Spirit leads into a

multitude of difficulties that might be
avoided. God sometimes has to protest
acts that are devoted but not according to His purpose.

Healing. Distinction made by Jesus
between sickness and demon possession.
Mk. 6:13.

Helping others. Gen. 40. Joseph a
blessing to his companions in tribulation by showing concern in their
troubles, and doing his best by God's
help to lift their burdens.

Heresy—The greatest. Jn. 6:28, 29.
Salvation by doing is the heart of every
ism. Christ's Gospel is one of "trust,"
not "try."

Higher Criticism. 1 Chron. 13. Laid
hand on the ark. Preachers who lay
hands on the doctrines of God's Word,
thinking to save Christianity from over-
throw. Dangerous to put unsanctified
hands on Christ—His virgin birth,
atonement, resurrection, etc.

Higher Criticism. Jericho theology,
the dry rot of the church. 2 Kgs. 2.
Sons of prophets air their doubts about
miracles (v. 16). Questioned literal
translation, so the Christ of some

preachers is but a ghost Christ. Theologians hindered Elijah, demanded critical investigation (v. 17). Elijah yielded to their clamor, but did not regain his power until he rebuked the false theologians (v. 18). Repudiate the Jericho theology (2 Tim. 4:2).

Higher Critics. Jn. 20:13. The complaint in many churches today—"They have taken away my Lord and I know not where He is."

Humility—Example of. Jn. 13. What was consistent with the dignity of Christ is much more consistent with ours, His servants. To serve in humility is the way to rule.

Hypocrites in church. Mk. 14:18. Hypocrites often crowd into the ordinances of the church in order to keep up with their reputation.

Hypocritical Professions. Acts 5. Beware of going to greater length in profession than the inner life will stand —of being ambitious to be counted religious and liberal while secretly cherishing selfish motives. This is lending oneself to the devil and is an affront to God.

Imitating others dangerous. Lk. 9:54. May do the thing Elias did and make a fool of yourself. Elias was sent when the world needed his peculiar methods.

Ingratitude. Lk. 17:11-19. Nine out of ten who benefit from Christ are unthankful. Love to Christ leads to thankfulness. Some are occupied more with their gifts than the Giver.

Ingratitude to God. Neh. 9. When seeking to God for mercy and relief in time of distress, it is good to stop and reckon up God's many mercies that we may see how ungrateful we have been. Will see that all glory belongs to God and all shame to ourselves.

Inheritance—Christian's. Josh. 13. The true Joshua, Christ, has opened up for us the gates of heaven, purchasing eternal inheritance for all believers. Like Joshua, He will in due time have the honor of putting them in possession of their inheritances.

Intercession. Gen. 18:23-33. Abram interceding for Sodom.

Intercession of Christ. Mt. 14:23, 24.

When disciples are at sea, their Master is at prayer for them.

Israel—Foreshadowed in Jonah. Like Jonah, out of their land, a trouble to Gentiles, cast out but miraculously preserved. In the future, in their hour of deep distress, they will cry to God, will be delivered and will go forth to the Gentiles as originally commanded, beseeching nations to be reconciled to God.

Israel—National restoration of. Mt. 24:32-35. Fig tree symbolic of Israel. In the days when Israel begins to bud again as a nation, the Lord's coming is near. Zionist movement a fulfillment. The word "generation" is elsewhere translated "race" or "people." Some interpret it that the generation living at the time the fig tree begins to bud, will not pass without seeing the culmination.

Israel—Pictured in Jacob at Haran. Gen. 29. Like Israel, he was out of place of blessing (Gen. 26:3). Without an altar (Hos. 2:4, 5). Gained an evil name (Gen. 31:1; Rom. 2:17-24) but under God's covenant care (Gen. 28:13, 14; Rom. 11:1, 25-30). Brought back ultimately (Gen. 31:3; 35:1-4; Ezek. 37:21-23).

Jews—Coming restoration of. Ex. 7:5. Their coming out of Egypt is a prophetic sign. The nations shall know Jehovah when He restores and blesses Israel in the kingdom (Is. 2:1-3; 11:11, 12; 14:1).

Jews—Dry bones vision. Ezek. 37. As bone came to bone, so the Israelites scattered over the earth will come to their respective tribes in the last days, when Christ will be recognized by them as their King.

Jews. Ex. 3. Burning bush pictures Israel in furnace, yet never consumed. God's relations with them are eternal (v. 15).

Jews—in millennium. Gen. 49. The cunning and often faithless Jacob comes forth at last in calm elevation of faith to bestow blessings and impart dignities. Israel's part in last dispensation, after Christ's return.

Jews. Gen. 43. **Benjamin here a type** of Christ as "son of sorrow." The Jews in Great Tribulation will plead for their Benjamin who has been lost

to them and in agony of the hour, He
will be revealed.

Jews. Gen. 44. Note Joseph's plan
to bring about full confession from his
brethren that they might have fellowship restored. So Christ, the antitype,
is dealing with His brethren the Jews.
His plan will culminate in great day of
confession in Great Tribulation when
they will both confess and mourn.

Jews. Gen. 45. Joseph pouring balm
into hearts of his brethren after their
days of testing, pictures coming scene
of Israel (Ezek. 22:19) when Christ will
be revealed. As they stand self-con-
demned before Him He will comfort
them (Zech. 31:1; 12:9) and will show
all to have been decreed for their
blessing (Rom. 11:11, 12).

Jews. Gen. 47. Joseph presenting
brethren in court—Christ in second advent presenting His brethren the Jews
in heaven's court, restoring them to
place of blessing in the earth. Jacob
blessing the king pictures Israel's portion in millennium, that of blessing
kings of the earth.

Jews—their banishment. Illustrated
in cities of refuge. Josh. 20. Israel

shed innocent blood and as the man-slayer has lost the inheritance and is banished. As long as priest, Christ, remains within the veil they will be kept out, but when He comes out, they will be forgiven. In the Great Tribulation anti-christ will be their pursuer and God will then provide a refuge for them (Rev. 12; Dan. 11:41).

Jews. Their condition pictured in book of Ruth. Jews backslide, leave the land, misery and death follow. An outcast Gentile girl finds the kinsman redeemer (church and Christ)—is married and later is the comfort of Israel.

Jews—Typified in Joseph's brothers who had previously rejected him. Gen. 42. The Jews, like these brothers, are passing through an age of tribulation which will culminate in the Great Tribulation, which will bring them to the feet of the One whom they crucified.

Judging Others. Job 8. The injustice of arguing that merely because one is in deep affliction, he is therefore a hypocrite. A day is coming when the secrets of God's dealings with His saints will be solved to universal satisfaction.

Judgment—Believer saved from.
Gen. 6. True believer floating in peace
on very waters by which wicked world
is judged.

Judgment. Gen. 6. Ark, type of
Christ as refuge of His people from
judgment (Heb. 11:7). Believer's safe
position in Christ. Word translated
"pitch" (v. 14) is same word translated
"atonement" in Lev. 17:11.

Judgment. Gen. 3:8-10. Sinners
outside of Christ will be conscious of
nakedness before God in judgment and
will cry for rocks and mountains to fall
on them and hide them from God's
presence. Only hope of standing before God is to be clothed in righteousness of Christ.

Kindness. David's kindness to Mephibosheth. 2 Sam. 9. David seeks
out Mephibosheth. The most necessi-
tous are generally the least clamorous.

Judgment—of the Cross. 2 Kgs. 2:8.
Jordan means "judgment." Christ and
the believer go through the judgment
of the cross together. Gal. 2:20; Rom.
6:3.

Kindness—Thankfulness to God for.

Acts 28 :11-15. If friends are kind, thank
God who makes them so.

Law and Grace—Contrast. Ex. 19 :5,
etc. Note that what under law was
conditional, under grace is freely given
in Christ to every believer. God in a
thick cloud, unapproachable. Under
grace we "draw nigh to God."

Law and Grace—Contrast. Ex. 20.
Law proposes life and righteousness
as end to be obtained by practicing, but
proves at outset that men are in a state
of death (Ps. 5 :20; 7 :7, 13; 3 :20). Law
demands strength from those who have
none and curses them if they cannot
keep it. Gospel gives strength to those
who have none and blesses in the exhibition of it.

Law and Grace. Lk. 3 :36-39. Par-
able teaches the folly of trying to mix
law and grace.

Leadership—Getting others to work.
Ex. 18 :18-21. Better to get one hundred men to work than do one hundred
men's work. May be overdoing in well
doing.

Leadership — Responsibility of. 2
Chron. 33 :9. No one ever sins alone—

always involves others. See v. 16. One who has led people wrong must strive with greater zeal to lead others in right way.

Leadership — Woman's. Judges 4. Mark of apostasy in a nation when woman has to take place of leadership. Conditions in modern church—men make only conditional or partial response to God's call and He has to use woman, who is called for companionship, not fighting man's battles.

Lies beget lies. Jn. 18:27. A lie begets a lie until they come to generations.

Lord's Supper. Feast of Passover a type of. Lev. 23:4, 5. This feast was a memorial bringing the redemption of Israel into view. Redemption is the basis upon which all blessing rests. Typically stands for "Christ our Passover" (1 Cor. 5:7), whose blood was shed for remission of sins.

Lord's Supper. Like feast of tabernacles. Lev. 23:34-44. This feast was both memorial and prophetic. Memorial of Israel's redemption out of Egypt (v. 43). Prophetic of Israel's coming kingdom-rest (1 Cor. 11:26).

Lost—The torments of the. Lk. 10:19-31. Sense of pain—tormented. Sense of memory—"Son, remember." Sense of loss—"seeth." Sense of fear—"Send him."

Love. Jonathan's for David. 1 Sam 20. Thinketh no evil (v. 2), not easily provoked (v. 8). Envieth not (v. 15). Seeketh not her own (v. 16). Believeth all things (v. 15, 16). Suffereth long, is kind (v. 24). Rejoiceth not in iniquity (v. 32).

Love of God for the wayward. Lk. 15:11-32. Father waits with open arms for wayward child. Would not let the prodigal brand himself permanently as one who had been an outcast (v. 22) but shut him up with kindness.

Love to Christ. Jn. 12:1-8. Mary's uncalculating love compared to Judas' calculating prudence. Any sacrifice for Christ's sake that will deepen our love for Him will increase our gifts to the poor.

Love to Christ. Lk. 7:41-50. The Christianity that minimizes sin and has nothing to say about pardon does not produce ardent love for Christ. Better be a redeemed outcast filled with intense love than a cold moralist.

Love to men. Lk. 10:30-37. Disregards race, creed, social standing—sees needs of men and goes to the aid of those who are suffering, in the spirit of Christ. Any person in need is our "neighbor."

Lying. Gen. 20. A lie is the handle that fits all the tools of sin. Truth stretched sure to fly back and hit one.

Lying Wonders. Ex. 7. The counterfeit manifestations of the magicians (Rev. 13:15). "Form of godliness without the real power thereof." Could only imitate in three things. Serpents (7:12). Blood (7:22). Frogs (8:7). When it came to exhibition of life, they failed.

Man—his wayward course. Gen. 1 finds man in beautiful Eden. Gen. 50 leaves him in a coffin in Egypt.

Man's extremity—God's opportunity of helping and glorifying Himself. Ex. 4:6. God's covenants are as firm as truth can make them. Trust Him whatever the outward circumstances.

Marriage. Gen. 24. God is ready to

lead in details of our lives. Marriage may be according to His will and Word and leading of the Holy Spirit.

Martyrs—Welcomed to heaven. Acts 7:54-60. When Jesus ascended, He sat down in heaven (Col. 3:1). Stephen sees Him standing. He welcomes to heaven the first martyr.

Materialism. Gen. 13. Lot's material blessings accompanied by moral blight.

Mistakes—Duty of confessing. Acts 23:5. If we are close to Christ, will be ready to confess mistakes lest it be a stumbling block to weaker brethren.

Memory—Immortal. Lk. 16:19-31. "Son, remember." May not "this flame" signify the anguish of memory —opportunities lost and sin committed?

Mourning—Dangers of. 2 Sam. 18:19-33. There is a mourning that blinds to blessings and duties. Don't let affections be bound up in one you cannot esteem on Christian grounds.

Murmuring. Ex. 16. Shows how a thousand mercies are forgotten in presence of one trifling privation. If God withdrew His protection every time we forfeit it by murmuring, where would we be?

Needs — Financial — Supplied. Mt. 17:24-27. If identified with Christ, He will, if we trust Him, supply temporal needs in mysterious ways. Note that one piece of money was shared.

Needs—Temporal. God the provider of. 1 Kgs. 17. God may use unlikely caterers (v. 6). If in God's way, may count on Him to supply every need. Faith puts God between us and circumstances that are against us. Living from hand to mouth all right if it is from God's hand to our mouths (v. 16). Our supplies multiplied, not in hoarding but in giving.

New Birth. Jesus' conversation with Nicodemus. Jn. 3.

Oebdience—Partial. Gen. 34. God had directed Jacob to Bethel. He went to Shechem. Partial obedience brings much trouble to Christian families. Daughters got mixed up with world and fell into a snare.

Obedience—Partial. 1 Sam. 15. Some judge many things in their lives but spare one Agag which the Lord has con-

demned. Partial obedience spells dis-
obedience and in absence of perfect
obedience our sacrifices are worthless
(v. 23).

Obedience to God. 2 Kgs. 5. Little
hope for one who is more concerned
about his dignity than his disease. No
results apart from implicit obedience
to God's requirements. Humble yourself and walk in the light of God's
commands.

Obedience to Christ. Jn. 2:1-12.
Those who expect favors from Christ
must observe His orders with implicit
obedience. If we follow Him, we will
fare with Him.

Opinions—Human. 2 Kgs. 5:11-14.
Things of God seem too simple for some
highly cultured intellects. 2 Cor. 11:3.
"I thought" (v. 11). Better let God do
the thinking. Hell, the only place
where men can think for themselves.
Naaman would have perished but for
servants not possessed of great intel-
lect.

Opportunities always at hand. Mk.
3:10. We will not be in want of opportunities for service if possessed of

power to satisfy the deepest human needs.

Opportunity—Failure to grasp. Ex. 4:14-18. Excessive timidity becomes unbelief and brings God's displeasure and withdrawal of opportunities. Others get the reward we might have had.

Opportunities — Opened in strange ways. Acts 23-26. When men think they are blocking the gates of the Gospel, God is opening them. Paul, as result of his trials, gets chance to preach the Gospel to men in high places.

Peace—Heart. 2 Chron. 15:15. If God has the heart, we have His rest. A little religion is a painful thing.

Peace—Jesus the source of. Lk. 8:22-25. He is the pacifier of tumults without and within.

Persecution. Acts 5:12-42. Good work for Christ never goes on but it is met by opposition. The destroyer of men will ever be an adversary to those who are true benefactors to men. We may cheerfully trust God with our safety.

Persecution. Acts 4. Persecution

gives wings to the truth. Let Satan's
agents be ever so spiteful, Christ's witnesses must be resolute. Holy Spirit
may be counted on to enable us to do
our part.

Persecution—Religious. Dan. 6. That
which we do faithfully in conscience toward God may be represented as done
with obstinate motives. Daniel willing
not only to strike for religion but to be
struck for it. Let God clear up your
integrity. Shutting mouths (v. 22) is
God's specialty.

Persecutions — Rejoicing in. Acts
16:24-29. Though called upon to suffer much for Jesus' sake, may be sure
God will in some way get glory to Himself by our testimony and persecutions.

**Persecution—Suffering, for Christ's
sake.** 1 Sam. 22:23. Those who honor
Christ, the true David, must expect to
share in His suffering and rejection.

Plans—Human. Folly of. 2 Kgs.
6:8-17. Plan without God and find
God's plan athwart yours (v. 8). Prov.
21:30. Better to have an ear for the
man of God (v. 10).

Poverty. Not a hindrance in God's

work. Acts 3. Empty pockets may go
along with true wealth (v. 6). Poor
churches are more often the miracle-
working churches. Rich churches
usually without power to say, "Arise
and walk."

Popular Opinion—Uncertainty of.
Acts 28:5, 6.

Power in testimony. I Kgs. 18. Necessity in public testimony of constantly humbling oneself before God (v.
36-38). Give God all the glory. Those
who bow lowest in God's presence can
stand straightest in presence of enemies
of God.

Power for service—in the Holy Spirit
and the Word. 1 Sam. 17:40. Living
water symbol of the Spirit in activity
(Jn. 7:38). Stones, instrumentalities
furnished—out of the brook. Word is
the instrument furnished by the Spirit.
By this He operates in power (1 Cor.
2:13; 2 Tim. 4:2).

Power in service. Judges 16. Samson's power not in his hair but in his
Nazarite consecration of which his long
hair was the badge. By losing the
badge he forfeited the strength.

Power in service—Lack of. Mt.
17:14-21. When the Man of prayer
came, the demon left the man. Danger
of having language of Jesus on our lips
without His power in our lives. Trouble
in the private life. Faith for casting
out demons not born in a crowd and in
the rush.

Praise. Acts 16:24-29. Need never
lack for matter for praise (Eph. 5:20).
Such a trial would put many Christians
out of tune.

Praise—Testifying of God's power.
Ex. 18. When God has led us through
the wilderness with victory, it is our
part to give Him the praise of what He
has given us the joy of and to let even
unbelievers know what is the power
that is with us.

Prayer—Access in. Esther 4:11.
Nothing bars us from the court of our
King in time of need. Welcome in the
very holiest through the blood of Jesus.

Prayer—as a heart preparation. Acts
16:12-15. Conversion of Europe began
here with a handful of praying women.
Prayer leads to an open heart. Even

the first disposition to accept truth is a
work of divine grace.

Prayer—Brings vision of the lost.
Acts 10:9. Takes prejudice out of the
heart (v. 14, 15.) Attend school of
Christ to know how to win souls.

Prayer—by a nation's ruler. Solomon, 1 Kgs. 8. Great thing when a nation's ruler can be led of the Spirit in
prayer and when he realizes all answer
to prayer is only on ground of shed
blood (v. 22, 62; Heb. 9:22; 10:19-20).

Prayer—changes things. 2 Kgs. 19.
If motive of prayer is God's honor, He
will graciously and copiously answer.
Hezekiah's prayer and the answer.

Prayer—Cold. Cannot get warm answers. Lk. 18:9-14. Cannot pray when
clothed with dead formalism instead
of humility.

**Prayer—Counting on Christ's will-
ingness.** Mk. 9:14-29. Those who are
beyond the power of the greatest men,
can be helped by the word of Jesus.
Need not even miss the blessing because
of the powerlessness of some in the
church.

Prayer—Counting on Christ's willing-

ness. Mk. 9:14-29. Prayer is not conquering God's reluctance but laying hold of His willingness (v. 22, 23). "If" hinders more than any other word.

Prayer—Definite transaction with Christ. Jn. 4:46-54. Note the answer to the prayer of the nobleman was not a mere coincidence (v. 53). Jesus speaks in heaven and it is done.

Prayer—Delay in answers to. Dan. 10. Failure to complete transactions with God may be responsible for unanswered prayer. When we rightly understand the methods of God's providence and grace concerning us, we will be reconciled to delays.

Prayer—Delays in answer to. Jn. 11. Jesus' delays in answering some prayers are not necessarily denials (v. 5, 6). May delay because He loves us, and always for His own glory. Trust Him, though you cannot understand His dealings.

Prayer. Ex. 30:34-38. **Incense, a type of.** See Ps. 141:2. Prayer of contrite believer ascends as a fragrant cloud to God (Prov. 15: 8). Fire under altar brought out fragrance (**Rom.**

8:26, 27). Fire was from blood-sprinkled altar (Heb. 10:19, 20). Prayers
were based on intercession of a priest
(Rom. 8:34).

Prayer for preachers. Mk. 1:35.
Preachers who are great thinkers must
be the greatest of prayers. Nothing is
so dead as dead orthodoxy.

Prayer—Satanic opposition to. Acts
16:16. Satan likes to ruffle us when
about to engage in prayer.

Prayer—for suffering saints. Acts
12. Times of public distress should be
especially praying times for the church.
However God's people are surrounded,
there is always a way open heavenward.
Strongest bars cannot intercept God's
power.

Prayer for those in authority. Ezra
6:1-10. Wise men in authority will not
despise the meanest saints who know
how to approach God on the ground of
the shed blood.

Prayer—God's acceptance of. 2
Chron. 6-7. Surest evidence of God's
acceptance of our prayers is descent of
His holy fire upon us. God thus owns
us as living temples.

Prayer—in times of difficulty. Dan. 6. Daniel looks away from circumstances to an omnipotent God. Some would call it prudence to omit prayer or to do it secretly under these circumstances.

Prayer—Mysterious agencies used in answering. Acts 12:7-11. Note economy of miraculous power. See v. 12. Reliance on divine power should not make us neglect ordinary means.

Prayer—National. The distresses of a nation (Neh. 1) should deeply concern the Christian and move him to earnest prayer for the nation. Note v. 8—our best pleas in such prayer are those founded on the Word.

Prayer—Need of completing transactions with God. Lk. 18:1-8. Prayer is not eloquence but earnestness.

Prayer—Offered to men. Lk. 18:9-14. Some make prayer a pretext to parade their own virtues.

Prayer—Power of, for God's people. Esther 4-6. If we have power with God in prayer, will find favor with men. God can turn the hearts of men which way He pleases.

Prayer—Preparing for answer to.
2 Kgs. 3:16-20. Have the ditches ready
to receive the water which God will
send through unseen channels.

Prayer—Persistence in. Lk. 11:5-10.
No modesty would cause the man to
stop asking for bread. Jesus would
have us ask definitely, earnestly and
with perseverance. Our prayers are
God's opportunities to do for us what
He could not otherwise do.

Prayer—Right motives in. 1 Kgs. 3.
Note purpose of Solomon's request (v.
9) that he might discern and judge, to
make himself useful to others. Wanted
delicate perception of sin so he could
discern good and bad. Before asking
anything he acknowledged past blessings (v. 6).

Prayer—Surprise at answers to. Acts
12:14-17. Believers are often slow to
believe when they see the answer to
their prayer. Cf. v. 5—faith to pray
without ceasing, yet marvel at the answer.

Prayer—The narrowness of our. Lk.
15:11-32. The prodigal's petition was
"Make me a servant." Place in the

household as a child was a blessing too bright for his thought. Effect of the father's embrace was to raise his expectation and prayer and give him the royal spirit of a son.

Prayer—The time for. Mk. 6:41. In all your hurry to get the Gospel to a dying world, take time where Jesus did.

Prayer—Unavailing. Lk. 18:9-14. Pharisee's prayer was more soliloquy than prayer. Prayed "with himself." Not conscious of any need. Thought only of himself. God did not regard him.

Prayer—Way of approach always open. (Neh. 2). We are not limited to certain moments in our addresses to the King of kings. Have access to His throne in every time of need.

Preaching. A model sermon. Acts 2:14-47. Preached by a man who had never attended a seminary, had been weak in himself, but is now filled with the Spirit and the Word. Note his positiveness (v. 14)—not "methinks" or "it seems to me."

Preaching—Fearless. Acts 7. Those filled with the Holy Ghost cannot but speak boldly against sin and will be made fit for anything.

Preaching—Expository. 2 Chron. 15:3. Doctrinal expository messages the backbone of the pulpit and essential to growth of the people. See v. 9. Get on fire of God and men will come to see you burn.

Preaching—John, a model preacher. Lk. 3. Preached judgment on sin and fruitlessness (9:17). Heart repentance, condition of forgiveness (v. 8). Holy living, evidence of true repentance (v. 8, 11, 14). Coming Savior and necessity of faith in Him (Acts 19:4). Dignity of service (v. 16). Baptism of Holy Spirit. Eternal blessedness of the saved (v. 17).

Preaching — One-handed. 1 Chron. 12:1-2. Could hurl stones with left as well as right hand. Able to give the unexpected blow. See v. 8 and cf. 2 Tim. 2:15; Eph. 6:12-19. Preachers who shoot blank cartridges.

Preaching—Outdoor. Acts 16:12-15. Greatest victories of the cross have been in outdoor meetings.

Preaching—Reproving sin. Nathan

reproving sin in high places. 2 Sam.
12. May have cost him nights of pain
and prayer to do it. Dogmatic message (v. 7) is truer and more tender
than soft speeches that do not arouse
conscience.

Preaching—Successful. I Sam. 3:19.
Samuel was born in answer to prayer
and a walking witness to power of
prayer. Prayer puts the preacher's
sermon into his heart and into the
hearts of the people.

Preaching. Summary of Elijah's
ministry. 1 Kgs. 17-21. Man of faith
(ch. 17), courage, earnestness (ch. 18),
resignation (19:15). Boldly denounc-
ed evil (ch. 21). Tenderness (17:19).
Prayer (18:36). Loyalty to God (17:1,
8; 21:17).

Preaching—The way John preached.
Lk. 3. Outspoken (v. 7). Easily under-
stood (v. 9, 11). Adapted himself to au-
dience (v. 12, 13, 14). Fearless (v. 19).
Exalted Christ, hid himself (v. 16).
What he got (v. 19, 20).

Preaching—Use of God's Word in.
Neh. 8. Right reading of Bible in
Christian assemblies is a means of hon-

oring God and edifying the church. Should be read distinctly and with the understanding.

Pride—False—refuses to bow to God's requirements, 2 Kgs. 5:11-14. Naaman wanted to be treated as a great man who happened to be a leper, rather than as a leper who happened to be great. Sets up his thoughts against God's. Be willing to wash in a ditch if God says so, or will miss the blessing.

Procrastination—Danger of. Ex. 4:21. One who resists light of divine testimony shuts himself up to judicial blindness and hardness of heart. Pharaoh had light but shut his eyes to it, therefore God hardens his heart.

Profession and Possession. Tares and wheat. Mt. 13:24-30. Tares a counterfeit. Appearance fair to eye. Lack of kernel not manifest until harvest time. True believers, the real wheat, rooted in Christ.

Professors and Possessors. Mt. 25. Wise virgins with oil in lamps (oil type of Holy Spirit). Those without oil speak of professors of religion who carry lamp (Bible) but are not regenerated.

Professors (not possessors). Ex. 12:38. Mixed multitude stands for unconverted church members whose presence is a source of weakness and division.

Promises of God—sure. Mk. 4:35. Our prospects are as bright as the promises God has made us. Jesus said, "Let us pass over." It was therefore an unsinkable ship.

Promotion—of God. Esther 2. God can raise up the poor out of the dust to set them among princes if He has a purpose to serve by it. If we first make sure of God's favor, we will find favor with men in so far as it is good for us and the purpose of God.

Protection—Divine. Acts 23:12-35. Satan-inspired men may write and vow against Christianity, but God has instruments they little dream of that He can use to defeat them.

Providence. An instrument in God's hands. 2 Sam. 18:7-9. God not tied down to human means. Nature fights for us when we are in God's will.

Providence—God's. Gen. 45. The trials of Joseph and his brethren shown to have been decreed of God for their blessing.

Providence of God. Illustrated by story of book of Esther. God takes a real interest in all our affairs and shapes His providences to work out His glory through them.

Providence—Ordered for the best. Acts 23:11. "Thou must bear witness." Secular events are often ordered to give us opportunity to witness. Paul's trials resulted in the spread of the Gospel.

Providence—Protecting. Ex. 2. Miraculous preservation of babe Moses. Note how (v. 10) the devil was foiled by his own weapon, by Pharaoh having to house the one who would deliver Israel. Nothing with God is accidental.

Providence—Purposes of. Acts 28. Wherever the Christian is put, he is placed there to do a work for Christ. Blessings may come to thousands as the result of a calamity in which God's children have suffered with others.

Providences—Hard. Ex. 1. God's dealings with His people at times seem

to thwart His promises. He tries faith
that His power might be magnified.
Sustains us in our trials if we trust.

Providences of God. Judges 14. Samson's riddle. When God brings good
out of evil to the followers of Christ—
when that which has threatened their
ruin turns to their advantage—then
comes meat out of the eater and sweetness out of the strong.

Providences—Seemingly trivial, often
play a big part in God's program. 1
Sam. 9:20. The losing of Saul's asses
was no mere accident. Slight incidents
may be means of linking us up to great
things.

**Prudence—Human—The insufficiency
of.** Acts 27:11. Worldly men insist on
being guided by human prudence, but
the Christian in communion with Jesus
the great Pilot, may know more about
the situation than a skilled heathen.

Purpose of heart. Dan. 1. Daniel was
not self-assertive or arrogant in his
fidelity to God, but as prudent as he
was brave. Determined to have a stand-
in with God first—later gets a stand-in
with the King.

Purpose of God—cannot be frustrated. 2 Kgs. 11. All attempts to frustrate it bound to fail. Though the promise of God is bound up in one life, yet will it not fail.

Purpose of God. Esther 4. We should study to find out for what end God has put us in the place where we are serving, and plan our lives to that end lest our opportunity slip.

Rebuking wrong in others. 2 Chron. 26:16-20. Withstand to the face those who are wrong, regardless of their reception of it. Gal. 2:11. Uzziah was great but not great enough to tolerate a rebuke. Should be thankful for remonstrances.

Reckoning—Day of. Esther 7:7. The day is coming when those who have persecuted and hated the followers of Christ would gladly be beholden to them, like the rejected virgins (Mt. 25) who cry, "Give us oil."

Reconciliation of enemies. Jacob and Esau. Gen. 33. To be reconciled to, is better than conquering an enemy. Victory may deprive enemy of his poison, but reconciliation of the will to do harm.

Rejection of Christ—Foolishness of. 1 Kgs. 10. In Mt. 12:42 Jesus mentions the queen of Sheba's inquiry after God through Solomon as showing the stupidity of those who would not enquire after God through Himself, who was "God manifest in the flesh" and therefore better able to instruct them than anyone else.

Rejection of Christ—The ingratitude of. Lk. 14:16-24. The ingratitude of those who slight the Gospel invitation is an abuse of His mercy. Grace despised is grace forfeited.

Remembrance—of God's blessings. Josh. 4. Value of devising some means to especially remember God's past works of wonder on our behalf, that our faith might be strengthened in the future.

Remembrance of God's past dealings, essential to success. Deut. 8. Touch on Israel's experiences in the wilderness and show the ways of God's providence and grace. Remembrance of past experiences of faith encourages faith to trust Him now and prevails upon us to serve Him cheerfully.

Remembrance of past sins. Deut. 9. Value of occasionally reviewing our past life of sin that we may see how much we are indebted to God's marvelous grace in Christ, and that we may humbly own that we never merited anything but God's wrath.

Repentance, False. Gen. 27:38. Difference between remorse and repentance. Esau weeps because of his lost advantage. See Heb. 12:17.

Repentance—Must be linked to sacrifice. 2 Chron. 29. Repentance cannot bring peace unless connected with the sin offering, Christ (v. 22). In confessing sin, approach God by the blood-sprinkled way (1 Jn. 1:7).

Resisting God—Results of. Ex. 5. Proud boast of a worm of the dust. God lets Pharaoh wrestle with frogs, lice and flies.

Resisting God's plan. Gen. 32:24-32. Jacob, a wrestled-with man. His confidence in the flesh was strong. Angel touches the seat of his strength to bring him to end of himself. When we are weak then we are strong (v. 26).

Responsibility of Christians. Acts 27. What Paul was to those in the ship, Christians should be in the world. Show the world the power of Christ. A praying, believing man can be the true captain of the ship if he will assume his rightful place.

Responsibility to God. Lk. 12:16-21. He plans foolishly who leaves God out of his plans. Some think they have only themselves to reckon with (v. 18).

Resurrection. Typified in the feast of first fruits (Lev. 23:10-14). Typical of Christ's resurrection, also the believer's (see 1 Cor. 15:23; 1 Thess. 4:13-18).

Rewards—Loss of. Gen. 19. Saved so as by fire (1 Cor. 3:11-15). Lot a type of the Christian who will get into heaven having suffered the loss of everything but his salvation.

Resurrection—of Christ. Judges 15:13-14. Samson bursting the bands illustrates the way Jesus was loosed from cords of death and came forth from tomb free of His grave clothes. Thus also He triumphed over powers of darkness.

Riches—Danger of. Mk. 10:23-31. Riches must be held subject to God's will and given up at His bidding. Can't trust God and "trust riches" (v. 24).

Riches—The hindrance of. Mt. 19:16-26. Nothing less than almighty grace of God can enable a man taken up with riches of world, to get into heaven. Riches, if under our feet, are stepping-stones, but if upon our backs are a curse. We may have great possessions or they may have us.

Righteousness of Christ. Coats of skins, Gen. 3:21. Christ made unto us righteousness—divinely provided covering to make fit for God's presence.

Righteousness of Christ—essential to salvation. Mt. 22:11-14. Wedding garment type of. Rom. 3:22; Is. 61:10; Rev. 19:7, 8; Eph. 4:24; Rom. 10:1-3.

Righteousness of Christ. Lk. 15:11-32. Covers the rags of our unworthiness. The father supplied the son with the new robe before taking him to his table, although he could kiss him in his rags. Had son provided his own robe it would not have been grace.

Ritualism—Powerlessness of mere. 1

Sam. 4. Israelites who had estranged themselves from the vitals of religion, are here seen putting their confidence in mere rituals of religion, hence soon find themselves with only a form of godliness but without the power thereof. Some today carry Bible under arm and even shout for religion but are without real communion with God.

Sabbath—Right use of. Lk. 6:1-5. A day to be spent in the service of, and to the honor of, Him who is Lord of the Sabbath.

Salvation—an experience. Jn. 9. Experience of Christ's saving power is a safer teacher than reason. Those whose eyes have been opened can be bold to witness of His saving power to a world that would explain it away.

Salvation—by grace. 2 Sam. 9. Story of David and Mephibosheth illustrates salvation by grace. Grace comes to the helpless, those "sold under sin." Invites us to place of peace and satisfaction. Feasts us at God's table. Keeps our lame feet out of sight.

Salvation—Coming near to. Acts 26:28, 29. "Almost," the saddest word in the English language. The measureless distance between "almost" and "altogether."

Salvation—Coming short of. Mt. 13: 1-23. Hearing but not heeding the Word (4, 19). Heeding for a time but not holding (5, 20). Holding but not hoeing out (7, 22). Wise hearers understand, heed, accept, hold fast, and pray for more light (v. 9).

Salvation—Counting the cost of. Lk. 14:28-33. Be willing to bid goodbye to things of the world or can never enjoy salvation.

Salvation—Divine movements in. Acts 10. A praying man, v. 2. Angel messenger, v. 3. Praying apostle, v. 9. Heavenly vision, v. 11. Preparation for message, v. 34. Preaching of the Word, v. 34. Regeneration, v. 44.

Salvation—Duty of coming to Christ. Lk. 9:51-62. Spiritual duty should have precedence over laws of propriety. The tenderest ties are subordinated to claims of Jesus. Be undaunted by hardship (58), unhindered in obedience (59, 60).

Salvation—even for those who have persecuted God's witnesses. Acts 16:

24-40. In the same hour, this jailer was
a brutal heathen, an anxious inquirer,
a rejoicing believer, and a Christian
worker.

Salvation—Evidences of. Acts 3.
Leaping up (v. 8)—quickened by the
Spirit (Eph. 2:5). Stood (v. 8).
Strength received (Eph. 6:13, 14).
Walked (v. 8)—progress (2 Cor. 5:7).
Entered with them (v. 8)—fellowship
(1 Cor. 12:12, 13). Leaping (v. 9)—joy
of salvation. Praising (v. 9) (Heb.
2:12).

Salvation. Ex. 27. Ark and altar.
Sinful man cannot approach God at the
ark (Heb. 9:8), but God approaches
man as a sinner through Christ (altar).
Blood prints all the way from ark to
altar. Only safe in God's courts when
redeemed on that path.

Salvation—Finding Christ. Mt. 2.
Following star to Christ. Light of
Scripture and light of nature. If followed, lead seeking souls to Christ in
whom there is joy unspeakable.

Salvation for all. Acts 10. Through
the finished work of Christ the door of
the Gospel has been opened to ''Who-

soever believeth.'' Whatever nation
one may be of, it is no prejudice to him
if he will receive God's appointed sacrifice.

Salvation—for the humble. Lk. 18:
9-14. What one may have and yet be
lost and what one may lack and yet get
saved.

Salvation—for the worst criminals.
Acts 9. No need to despair of the conversion of those who commit the worst
outrages against Christianity. Jesus
can break down the most stubborn will.

**Salvation—for those willing to re-
ceive.** Jn. 5. Jesus delights to help
the helpless and manifests His mercy
toward those who are willing to be
helped. Can overrule the powers of
nature on behalf of trusting souls.

Salvation. Gen. 3:6-15. Adam and
Eve conscious of nakedness before God
because of sin. Tried to cover nakedness by own efforts but could not be at
peace with the best they could do. God
comes seeking them as Christ, in grace,
came to seek and save the lost. God
by His own hand covers their nakedness and then only could they be satis-

fied. The covering procured only after the shedding of blood.

Salvation. Gen. 11. Cannot be secured by building tower of self-righteousness up to heaven. Must have a foundation laid in heaven by God Himself. Man at his best outside of Christ, builds "under the heavens."

Salvation. Gen. 6. Christ the ark of safety. Noah's salvation was not his own invention but was revealed by God (v. 13).

Salvation—not of our own merits. Lk. 15:11-32. The father did not condition his son's home-coming upon his going to work. He may have worked afterward, but not to obtain entrance to the father's house.

Salvation of loved ones. Mt. 15:21-28. Concern for her daughter who was in Satan's power. A believing, praying mother takes her in prayer to Jesus and gets complete deliverance for her. Child-like faith of the mother overcame serious obstacles.

Salvation—Process of. Jn. 4:6-39. Those who come face to face with their own helplessness and sin and give their hearts to Jesus, will be the recipients of living waters that will quench the thirst of the soul.

Salvation—Process of. Lk. 19:1-10. Note Zaccheus' curiosity, v. 4, followed by conviction, v. 6, and consecration, v. 8.

Salvation—Procuring of. Mt. 13:44. Jesus the buyer of the field at awful cost (1 Pet. 1:18). Israel hidden in the world, the treasure (Ex. 19:5; Ps. 135: 4) for the sake of which He bought field. Used also of all sinners, for God so loved the WORLD (Jn. 3:16).

Salvation—Rejection of. Mt. 22. Gospel call bids all to the feast. Some don't want to go to heaven, and invent excuses for rejection of Christ. Some think to intrude in the rags of their hypocrisy. The humble gladly accept the invitation and are satisfied.

Salvation—Satan's opposition to. Mk. 1:21-28. When Jesus is preached to a soul, the devil rages. Won't give up his victim without a struggle. Even demons can be orthodox (v. 24). Demon-possessed man may be orthodox, yet lost.

Salvation—Steps in. Illustrated by

X Naaman. 2 Kgs. 5. Hear, assent, come, forsake own thoughts, accept God's thoughts, take place of a sinner, made clean.

Salvation—Steps in. Jn. 1:35-51.
X Hearing of Christ as Lamb of God (v. 36). Following (v. 37). Testifying of (v. 41). Looking upon (v. 36). Abiding with (v. 39). Winning others (v. 42).

Salvation—Sufficient for any case. Acts 14:8-19. No hopeless cases with Christ. If one's spiritual lameness is cured by Christ, it will be manifested by holy exultation and walk.

Salvation—The first fruit of. Acts
X 9. See v. 20. A thoroughly converted man is bound to preach Christ as Son of God.

Salvation—The ground of. Mt. 7: 24-29. Jesus Christ and the Word the only sure foundation that can stand the judgment winds.

Salvation—Who may be saved. Lk. 16:19-31. Prosperity not a mark of being a favorite of heaven, nor poverty a mark of God's rejection of a man. Salvation is appropriated only by those who accept the evidence of God's Word during their lifetime. Having died outside of Christ, there is no ray of hope forever.

Satan—and the believer. Judges 16. Satan ruins men by rocking them to sleep, flattering them into good opinion of their own safety, then robbing them of their strength and honor, leading them captive at his will.

Satan's devices—to defeat God's people. 1 Sam. 11. Right eye is eye of faith. Left eye was covered with the shield when they went out to battle. By the proposed compromise Israelites would be unfitted to fight. Thus Satan tries to cripple us in service. Compromising saint is always blind in one eye.

Satan—His attempts to destroy Christ. 1 Sam. 18-19. The murderous attempts of Saul on the life of David, the anointed king, illustrates the repeated attempts of the usurper Satan against the life of Christ, the anointed One.

Satan—His hatred of Christians and Christian work. Lk. 8:26-39. Demon-possessed men never have expectation to receive benefit from Christ, or inclination to do Him service, a fact alone which proves His deity. Demons know Him to be the Son of God who is to execute vengeance.

Satan—His hatred of God's witnesses. Ex. 7. Satan's resistance to God's testimony of His Son is often offered by those who have a "form of godliness without the power thereof." Note that these magicians finally failed. Their tricks were "lying wonders" (Rev. 13:15).

Satan—His opposition to a soul seeking Christ. Ex. 5-12. Pharaoh a type of Satan. His efforts to keep Israel entangled in Egypt in one way or another, illustrate Satan's efforts to involve the believer in the world.

Satan—His power over saints. Job 1. His power always limited by the will of God. The way we stand under Satan's assaults reveals what we are. Satan's power over believers today is bounded by the intercessory prayer of Jesus.

Satan—His Tactics. Mt. 13:24-30. Sows tares on top of the wheat. Mixed multitude in the church. So great his power of deception that tares often really suppose themselves to be wheat (7:21-23). Note Satan's confidence in his sowing (went his way—no doubt as to results—v. 25).

Satan—His wiles in catching men. 2 Sam. 18: 1-9. Devil leads one on till he gets him caught and then takes away his support.

Satan's devices to trip believers. 1 Sam. 17:37-40. If world can't dissuade believers from opposing sin, tries to get them to fight in its own armor. Church is smothered by Saul's armor. Preachers wearing the forgings of criticisms.

Satan—Temporary power of. Ex. 4: 1-5. Rod, symbol of power in Christ's hand, was not wrenched from Moses' hand. He cast it down and it remained serpent only while out of his hand. Rod, temporarily out of Christ's hand, has taken serpent form, but Satan's power can be exercised only as long as Christ wills. He will stretch forth His hand and take sceptre and Satan's rule will be ended.

Scheming. Gen. 27. God not in need of our cunning or deceit to help out His purposes. Nothing gained by anxiety and planning of Christians.

Science. Gen. 4:22. First inventors descendants of Cain, not believing Seth. Leaders in science often infidels and despisers of God. Dangers of knowledge not accompanied by outpouring of grace.

Second Advent of Christ. Illustrated by Moses coming from mount. Christ, like Moses, went above (Acts 1:9), telling people to tarry. In His absence many forgot His promise to return and made themselves gods (2 Tim. 3:1-4; 4:3, 4; Mt. 24:12), denying His return (2 Pet. 3:3, 4). Jesus will come unexpectedly (Mt. 25:13), punishing evil doers (2 Thess. 2:7, 8) who are naked (Rev. 6:16, 17) and gathering the true to Himself (1 Thess. 4:13-18).

Second Advent of Christ. It tarries. 1 Sam. 13:11. Scoffers of last days think promise of Christ's return is broken because He does not come in their time. Abandon God's program and take religion in their own hands.

Second Coming—Denial of. Lk. 12:42-48. Effect of unbelief in Christ's

coming is worldliness and licentious-
ness. V. 45 is the theology of unfaith-
ful stewards who will be caught unawares in their shame.

Second Coming. Mt. 17. See in the
transfiguration a miniature picture of
the coming kingdom. Jesus in His
glory (v. 2). Moses stands for believers who have passed on through death
(v. 3). Elijah represents those who
will be translated (v. 3; 1 Thess. 4:14-
17). Three disciples represent Israel
in the flesh at His coming. Gentiles at
foot of mountain represent living nations.

Second Coming—Preparation for. Lk.
12:35-40. Loins girded—ready in service. Lights burning—ready in testimony. Those who are found active in
service at His coming will greatly rejoice.

Second Coming—Preparation for.
Mt. 25. Some in the church in the last
days will become drowsy and will be
taken unawares by Christ's coming.
Only those will be accepted who have
both lamp (Bible) and oil (Holy Spirit
in regeneration). No one else can im-

part the oil—each must get it direct through Christ before it is too late.

Sectarianism—Jesus' rebuke of. Mk. 9 :38-41. There is a subtle comfort in telling another man to sit down and keep quiet. This man was sincere and successful, not like the man in Acts 19 : 13-16. Do not forbid a man because he is unattached. V. 40 is limited by Mt. 12 :30.

Security in Christ. Josh. 2 :21, 22. Rahab's scarlet line speaks of the safety that comes to our households where the scarlet line of Christ's atoning work is exhibited through faith (Heb. 9 :19, 22).

Security of believer. Ex. 12. Israelites safe behind blood-marked door. Ate the roast lamb within in perfect peace, believing God's promise that if the blood was applied, the destroyer would pass over. No need for anxiety.

Security of believer. Gen. 7 :16. Noah and family safely in the ark—God shuts door from outside. Their safety depends on God, who will not let them fall out. Noah could only look up through window in top.

Self-confidence. 2 Chron. 26. The world's smiles are the devil's darts. Success is the ruin of many. Dangerous to be strong except in the Lord and the power of His might.

Self-confidence—Danger of. Mk. 14: 26-31. Boasting the first step in backsliding. Beware of uttering rash vows. Turn vows into prayers for strength. Easier to die a martyr than to live a hero.

Self-exaltation—abased. 2 Sam. 18. Never pays to take counsel against the Lord and His anointed. Absalom, seeking exaltation, got it by being lifted up between heaven and earth (v. 9).

Self-exaltation. Lk. 14:7-11. Pride will have a fall and will get shame to itself. Why some are not bidden to higher service for Christ. Prov. 15:33.

Self-exaltation—Penalty of. 1 Kgs. 1. When men try to exalt themselves, God sometimes leaves them to themselves until they are corrected with a scourge of their own making. God will be consulted.

Self-glory. 2 Kgs. 10:16. Aim at applause of men instead of honor of

Christ, and we are on a false bottom. An upright heart approves itself to God and covets no more than His acceptance.

Self—Exalted opinion of. Job 29. Speaks of himself fifty times. Cf. Ch. 42. Know God and you will be humble. If you really know yourself, you can't be proud. Job got on the devil's territory through self-righteousness. Man's uprightness consists first in owning himself a sinner.

Self-pity—Foolishness of. Job 3. "Pity thyself" is the devil's message to a Christian. Satan tries to embitter the saint against God by causing him to misunderstand God's providences. God's worst is better than the devil's best.

Self-Reformation—Worthlessness of. Mt. 12: 43-45. Some repent of sin, and swear off, but do not take step of saving faith which would bring in the Holy Spirit to occupy the garnished house. If Jesus is not received as Savior, door is left open for Satan's forces to return in greater power than ever.

Self-righteousness — Hindrance to salvation. Acts 9. If the greatest re-

ligionist and moralist who ever lived
had to come down the ladder of self-
righteousness before he could get saved, it is of no use for any man to go up.
The chief of legalists acknowledges
himself the "chief of sinners."

**Self-righteousness — The uselessness
of.** Lk. 18:9-14. No way of approach
to God on the ground of our own merits. Come only on the ground of God's
mercy.

Separation. Ex. 5-12. Satan always
seeking to get believers to compromise
with Egypt (the world). Be a Christian but stay in Egypt—or at least don't
come entirely out.

**Separation—Newness of life in
Christ.** Josh. 3. Passing of Jordan type
of Christian's death with Christ (Rom.
6:6-11; Col. 3:1-3). Passing from an
old world into a new life.

Separation. Num. 6. The Nazarite,
type of those who set out in path of
special devotion to Christ. Found all
their joy in the Lord. Long hair a vis-
ible sign of separation—willingness to
bear reproach for Jehovah's sake. Note
(v. 3) they were separate from things

which, though not sinful in themselves, might tend to hinder entire consecration (Heb. 12:1).

Separation—Power of. Gen. 14. Abraham gives the world the most effectual service by being separated from it.

Servants—God's ability to raise up. 1 Kgs. 17. God has power to raise up men in unlikely places and fit them for the work He designs them for. Can use one man to arrest downward movement of a nation and with no weapon but the Word and prayer marvelously provides for them in times of sore testing.

Service—Call to. Jonah 1. Men may be distinctly called of God to proclaim His message, yet refuse to obey. Indisposition to preach will not rid one of obligation to preach. God sends storms to teach wisdom of obedience.

Service—Call to. Lk. 10:1-12. Whom Christ sends He goes along with to give success. His messengers should apply themselves under deep concern for souls and not expecting comforts from the world.

Service—Call to. 1 Sam. 3. Child may have an ear for God's call and a message for God's bidding. God sometimes passes over ordained ministry and men of note and uses a mere lad as His mouthpiece. Mt. 21:16; 11:25; 1 Cor. 1:27.

Service—Consecration in. Ex. 4. God does not require great talent, but asks Moses to yield to Him the little that he has in his hand. Giving God the use of our small powers is what counts.

Service—Distraction in. Lk. 10:38-42. Word "cumbered" (v. 40) lit. "pulled this way and that." Kind of service that makes people cross with the Lord, is outcome of neglect of communion.

Service—Doing for others. Acts 9:36-43. Full of good works. The backs of the widows praised Dorcas (v. 39). Do we live, or merely talk good deeds?

Service. Eliezer the model servant, Gen. 24. Does not run unsent (v. 2-9). Goes where he is sent (4:10), does nothing else. Is prayerful and thankful (v. 12-14, 26, 27). Wise to win (v. 17, 18, 21). Speaks of his master, not himself (v. 22, 34-36).

Service—Exalting Christ in. Acts 9: 32-35. Peter takes the place of an instrument (v. 34). Do we put self in the foreground in our service, or Jesus Christ?

Service—Faithfulness in. Mt. 25: 14-30. Wise investment of talents for Jesus Christ. Not a question of great talents but of faithfulness in the use of those given to us. All have not same ability but have the same Lord and are responsible to serve Him with the same zeal.

Service for Christ—Trials of. Ex. 5. When called to God's service expect Satan's hatred. May be tried by threats of enemies, unjust censures of friends who judge by outward appearances.

Service—For new converts. Jn. 11: 41-44. Our part after men are raised from spiritual death is to release them from the grave clothes that have bound them. First help to roll away the stone (v. 41).

Service—Giving God the glory of. Acts 10. See v. 26. Don't accept honors that belong alone to God. Rev. 19: 10; 22:9; 2 Cor. 12:6.

Service—Giving God the glory of. Acts 14:8-19. Men are always ready to render to God's instruments the honors that belong only to Him. Guard the honor of Christ and turn all thoughts to Him.

Service—Guidance in. Acts 16:6-11. God sometimes guides by hindrances. Let the Holy Spirit open the door, or you court failure. Lose no time in going where God calls you.

Service—Humility in. 2 Chron. 2:4-6. Should go about every work for God with due sense of our utter insufficiency for it. In ourselves can do nothing adequate to the divine perfections.

Service—Importance of seemingly trivial. Acts 23:12-35. Paul's sister's son plays a minor part in the program, but a necessary one. If we can't be a Paul, we can be like Paul's sister's son, ready to do the next thing to us. A mere boy here defeats forty men who had vowed.

Service—in faith. Mt. 13:25. If we mix our seed-sowing with doubt, will get a crop of weeds. When the devil sows he has confidence in what he has planted.

Service. Must be done according to Scriptures. 2 Sam. 6. Bringing ark to Jerusalem on cart, imitating heathen example, instead of in the appointed way (Num. 4:1-15). Unscriptural service comes to grief eventually. God's work must be done in God's way.

Service—Opposition in. Ezra 4. God's work cannot be advanced but Satan and his followers rage. Do not dwell on the enemy, but keep an eye single to God, who will give the victory. Note v. 14. A secret enemy to God's work is often gilded over with a pretended affection for the government.

Service—Opposition in. Neh. 4. Reproaches of enemies of God's work should have the effect of quickening us to duty rather than driving us from it.

Service—Preparation for. Judges 6. Gideon. God calling His mightiest servants from places of obscurity and inspiring them with assurance of His presence.

Service—Preparation for. 1 Sam. 9: 25-27. Can't serve God until instructed of God. There is a time to be up and doing and a time to be still before God. Time spent in Word of God (v. 27) is a condition of real accomplishment for God.

Service—Preparation for. Those called to great service may expect for a time to be obscure. God gives special preparation at back side of the desert where the vision was made real.

Service—Qualification for. Acts 27: 23. "Whose I am" must come first. Some stop with "whose I am" and do not go on to "whom I serve."

Service—Qualifications for. Ex. 4:6, 7. Bosom stands for what we **are**— hand for what we **do**. The two signs, rod and hand, speak of preparation for service. Hand that holds rod of God's power must be a cleansed hand, swayed by a new heart.

Service—Qualifications for. Judges 7. Gideon's men. Prepared men to fight God's battles in God's way. One's unfitness for battle often seen in the unconscious trifling acts of life which betray uttter lack of faith and show that one's heart is not in the battle.

Service—Qualifications for. Judges 15. Samson in power of the Spirit slays one thousand with jawbone of an ass. Holy Spirit enables one to do the seemingly impossible even though there are only the most contemptible instruments at hand to work with.

Service—Responsibility to Christ in. Lk. 19:11-27. Christ has gone into far country to receive for Himself a kingdom and return. Has endued His followers in the world with advantages and capacities of serving Him until He returns. Will have to render account to Him and will be rewarded accordingly.

Service—Right spirit in. Mt. 20. One hour's service in spirit of humble trust will be as abundantly rewarded as twelve hours' legal service where reward is sought as a matter of debt. Jesus will in due time pay us what is right (v. 7). Those who try to call God to account (v. 12) will get the least.

Service—Readiness in. Acts 28. Be ready to do good wherever God's will carries you. Do you have the touch that gives life where you go? (v. 8.)

Service—The hireling spirit in. Lk. 15:25-32. Elder brother shows he had served in spirit of a hireling, or he would have enjoyed being merry with friends, rejoicing over brother who had come back home. At heart, he himself was a prodigal. Cf. v. 2.

Service—The secret of. Mk. 10:35-45. Reason so many fail in service, because they want honors instead of humble service (v. 44). The lowlier the service, the more exalted the greatness.

Service—to those in distress. Acts 28. Do we live, like Paul, to be of service to those in distress? Would we feel above gathering sticks? Be willing to do humble tasks in order to win men.

Service—True greatness in. Mt. 20:20-28. Way to true greatness in service is to be humble and serviceable with an eye continually to the great pattern Jesus, who came into world not to be waited on but to wait on others.

Service—Unfitness for. Mt. 12:9-14. Hand speaks of service. Withered hand speaks of paralysis in service. Many

Christians with withered hand because
of sin. Need the touch of Jesus to restore them.

Service—Value of method in. Mk. 6:
32-44. Perfect order of Jesus' work.
Perfect generosity and perfect economy.
Gifts from His hand not to be squan-
dered.

Service—Wisdom in. Lk. 16:1-12.
Worldlings are often more consistent
with themselves and more enthusiastic-
ally pursue their ends than Christians.
Though they aim low, they aim better,
improving their opportunities and doing that first which is more needed. Be
wise in spiritual affairs.

Service—Wasting time in. Neh. 6.
Let those who are tempted to waste
time by attending affairs to no real purpose for God, make use of the answer
in v. 3, ''We have work to do and cannot come down.''

Sickness. Greatness or goodness
cannot exempt one from sickness if it
is God's will, 2 Kgs. 20. Yet sometimes
when the death sentence has been received in the body, it is reversible
through Spirit-born prayer.

Sickness. Jn. 11. May be for the glory of God in manifesting Christ's healing power (v. 4).

Simony—Making money out of religion rebuked. Acts 8:9-25.

Sin—Blindness of. 2 Kgs. 6:18-23. Sin blinds the soul till nothing seems real. Led in its blindness into the enemy's camp.

Sin—Bondage to. Ex. 1. Bondage of Israel to Egypt a picture of sinner's bondage to the world. Can only be broken by trusting the God-sent deliverer.

Sin—Cleansing from. Ex. 30:17-21. Laver, type of Christ who cleanses from defilement (Jn. 13:2-10; Eph. 5:25-27). Priests could not approach the holy place till hands and feet were cleansed.

Sin—Cleansing from. Neh. 13:8. Those who would expel sin out of their hearts, the "living temples," must throw out its household stuff and all provision made for it. The blood of Christ may then be applied by faith.

Sin—Confession of. 1 Chron. 21. If we have sinned, safest thing to do is to flee to Christ, who is an altar and sacrifice (v. 18). Through Him alone can we win back the joy of salvation.

Sin—Confession of. 2 Sam. 12. David, blind to his own faults, condemns his own faults when he sees them in other people (v. 6). Is finally brought face to face with his sins and confesses. His fellowship with God restored, but God does not interfere with the consequences in his life (v. 11).

Sin—Conviction for. Gen. 3:12. God convicts of our own sin. Devil convicts us of others' sins.

Sin—Cure for. Moral lepers. Mt. 1: 40-43, need the touch of Jesus' cleansing hand. Some doubt His willingness who do not doubt His power. He says, ''I will'' (Jn. 6:37).

Sin—Downward steps of. Story of Saul. Parleying with sin (1 Sam. 13:8). Yielding and disobeying (13:9-14). Habitually yielding (15:9-23). Rejected of God (15:23-35; 16:14). Self-abandoned (28:6-20). Aiming to destroy others (18-24). Destroying himself (31:4-6).

Sin—Effect of, in the church. Josh. 7. Sin separates from God and if not put away brings disaster not only upon the sinner but associates. Story of Achan illustrates oneness of the church in Christ (1 Cor. 5:1-7; 12:12, 14, 26). Whole cause may be injured by unspirituality of one believer.

Sin—God's estimate of. 2 Sam. 24. David's sin in numbering the people, shows God does not judge of sin as we do. What appears small to us.

Sin—Its penalty returns. Esther 7. Mischief is sure to return upon the person himself who contrives it. Ps. 7:15, 16.

Sin—Its penalty sure to fall. 2 Kgs. 9:30-37. God doesn't always pay up for sin every week, but eventually He pays.

Sin—Leprosy a type of. Lev. 13. In the system, becomes loathsome, incurable by human means. Curable only through Christ's atoning work.

Sins—National. Judah in captivity, 2 Kgs. 24-25. The nation that has by sin provoked God to leave, may expect to be encompassed about with innumerable evils.

Sin—National. 2 Kgs. 17. Nation

that forgets God may expect to be forgotten of God. If men will not serve God in their own land, may be forced to serve enemies in a strange land.

Sin—Necessity of being armed against. 2 Kgs. 8:12, 13. Men often think themselves sufficiently armed against those sins which later completely overcome them.

Sin—Public confession of. 1 Sam. 7. Israel acknowledges that by sin they have provoked God to withdraw from them—make solemn business of returning to God and are assured of renewed prosperity. Note seven steps: v. 2. Lamented, v. 3. Exhorted, v. 4. Forsook sin, v. 5. Intercession, v. 6. Confession, v. 8. Supplication, v. 9. Sacrifice, Heb. 10:19.

Sin—pursues the sinner. 2 Sam. 3. Will overtake the sinner at last in one way or another. Illustrated both by Abner and Joab (v. 29).

Sin—Resulting from leisure. David's sin. 2 Sam. 11. Prosperity leads him up to a period of spiritual declension. The devil finds work for the idle. Sin started leads to more sin to hide it.

Even a man "after God's heart" may fall into gross sin.

Sin—Separating power of. Gen. 3: 10, 12. Consciousness of sin separates from God and destroys fellowship with those nearest to us.

Sin—Sorrows of. Ex. 7. Sin turns man's comforts into crosses. What is water today may be blood tomorrow.

Sin—sure to find one out. 2 Sam. 20: 12, 13. The covering of blood with a cloth cannot stop its cry for vengeance in God's ears. Sinners think themselves safe if they can conceal their acts from the eyes of the world.

Sincerity—False. 1 Kgs. 18:28, 29. Sincerity of no avail when off the track. Sincerity in a false religion leads to hell.

Sincerity—No evidence of right. Acts 26:9. May be sincere and yet the biggest fool on earth. Most inhuman acts have been done under color of religion. Misinformed conscience a dangerous thing.

Skepticism—laughs Jesus to scorn. Mk. 5:39-41. Some rely on reasonings of men rather than Word of God. Jesus had power of God on His side, the doubters did not. Skepticism is powerless to break up funerals.

Skepticism—The folly of. Jn. 9. The skeptics could not account for the change in a life by their theories (v. 16). The "how" of Christ's saving power is an unanswerable question. Experience is safer teacher than human reason.

Skepticism—The way to get rid of. Jn. 1:35-51. Be honest enough to go to Christ and put Him to the test.

Skeptics—The answer to. Acts 4:13-22. Put up a redeemed man and the skeptics can't explain how he got his legs. Saved men should be on hand when their testimony is worth something.

Socialism—The true. Acts 4:31-35. New-formed church, created a situation which called for extraordinary measures. Jewish converts were ostracized and deprived of work. Persecution drove these together and Christians helped supply needs. Modern socialism says, "What's yours is mine." Early Christians said, "What's mine is yours." A brotherhood founded on divine sonship—not the modern "universal brotherhood of man."

Sonship—Divine. Lk. 15:11-32. The eternity of. If one has really been in the Father's house as a son, he, like the prodigal, is still a son and will be constantly constrained by the Spirit to "arise and go home," if he wanders away.

Sorrow—Conquered by earnest prayer. Mk. 14:32-42. Cf. v. 40—disciples forgot in sleep. While saints slumber, sinners plot against Christ.

Soul-winner. The heart burden for the lost. Jesus leaves a crowd to deal with one man.

Soul-winner. The heart burdened for the lost. Lk. 19:41-44. If like Jesus, we would weep over sinners going madly to hell.

Soul-winners—The inspiration of. Jn. 20. A risen Christ. Haste characterized the resurrection day. Should haste in carrying the proclamation of salvation until Jesus comes.

Soul-winning—against odds. Acts 16:16-19. Turn hindrances to opportunities. Opposition brought them opportunities to witness for Christ.

Soul-winning. A thorough conversion is essential to success in winning others. Acts 9:32-35. Does our conversion make it easy to believe the Bible? (v. 35). Nothing can withstand argument of a changed life.

Soul-winning—Compassion in. Acts 3. The hand of compassion extended by men filled with the Spirit, in the name of Jesus Christ, is fraught with power to lift men heavenward.

Soul-winning—Duty of. Jn. 6:1-13. Those who have received the Bread of life are to be distributers of it to other hungry souls.

Soul-winning. Fishing for men. Mt. 13:48-52. Net of Gospel, cast into sea of humanity, gathers every kind. These remain together in the professing church until end of age. Note—no world conversion pictured here.

Soul-winning—Going after men. Mk. 2. Some men cannot come to Jesus on their own feet but must be carried by others on the stretcher of love, faith and perseverance. Exercise faith for those who do not have it (v. 5) until it is born in them.

Soul-winning. Going after the lost. Lk. 18:35-43. Note v. 40. Many are not saved because no one has "brought" them. Can't come to Jesus on their own feet.

Soul-winning—Hints for. Acts 3. Fastening eyes upon (v. 4)—give one dealt with exclusive attention. Look on us (v. 4). Get the man's attention. Silver and gold have I none (v. 6). Get rid of every subject but the one great one. Such as I have (v. 6). Introduce thought of eternal life. In the name of Jesus (v. 6). Get sinner to take definite step by faith. Took him by the hand (v. 7)—personal contact. Lifted him up (v. 7). Pray and pull is the combination of lifting men.

Soul-winning—Indifference of some toward. Jn. 5. Church members who pass by those daily who cannot get into the waters of salvation themselves.

Soul-winning—Joy of. Mt. 18:11-14. Definite soul-winning work, centered on individual rather than masses. Joy of bringing them home to God one by one.

Soul-winning—Natural fruit of salvation. Jn. 4:6-39. A city evangelized because of a conversation at a well (v. 29, 30). Listened to the woman's testimony because they saw the transformation in her (v. 39).

Soul-winning—Objectors to. Elder brothers in the church. Lk. 15:25-32. Have attitude of coldness toward prodigals brought in, and do not deeply join in Christ's longing for the wayward. Would feed the prodigals on cold potatoes instead of the fatted calf.

Soul-winning—Patience in. Lk. 9: 51-56. Do not show bitterness toward rejecters.

Soul-winning—Points in. Acts 8:26-40. Spirit-controlled—v. 26. Awake to chance to speak to one man—v. 27. Not afraid of one in higher social rank —v. 27. Friendly—v. 29. Know the Bible—v. 30. Thorough—v. 36.

Soul-winning — Requires personal touch. Acts 8:26-40. Angel spoke to Philip but message had to be taken to Ethiopian by a man, not an angel. Only those redeemed can effectually proclaim salvation.

Soul-winning—The call to. Mk. 1: 16-20. Jesus calls busy, never lazy men, to be His representatives. He "makes" His followers fishers of men. Jesus' training school for soul winners.

Soul-winning—The joy of. Lk. 15: 3-24. Note v. 5, 9, 10, 23, 32.

Soul-winning—The time for. Lk. 16: 28. The time to entreat men is while you are on earth. Can't help them afterward.

Soul—Value of. Mk. 5:13. Two thousand swine were suffocated that one soul might be saved.

Soul-winning—The process of. Jn. 1:35-51. The next thing to finding Christ as the Lamb of God is to find another and introduce that one to Him. One soul won is a link to hundreds more.

Spirit-filled Life. 2 Kgs. 2:9. Double portion of the Spirit. Christ gives double manifestation of the Spirit to believers: (a) Jn. 20:22, "breathed on them"—imparted divine nature (b) Acts 1:8, communicated power for service. Regeneration and fullness of the Spirit.

Spirit-filled Life. Pentecost. Acts 2. Waiting on God for the anointing of the Spirit is the condition of spiritual blessing and power for witnessing.

Spiritual Food—for theological student. 2 Kgs. 4:38-41. Feed on the wild gourds of the world and will find yourself in the grip of spiritual death. Meal made of bruised corn speaks of Christ in the Gospel. Put the results of the cross in the pot and it will take away the poison.

Spiritual Food. 1 Sam. 14:25-30. To fail to feed upon the honey (Christ in the Word) is not time gained but strength lost, unfitting one for conflicts.

Spiritualism. Condemned in an incident which leading spiritualists make frequent use of to support their beliefs (Mk. 9), claiming that Moses and Elijah were spirit manifestations. Incident teaches that Christ was exalted far above Moses or Elijah, and warns against seeking to any other but the Son of God Himself. Purpose of transfiguration to fulfill promise made to disciples to reveal Himself, they being depressed because of His announcement of 8:31. He shows them the power of His coming kingdom.

Spiritualism. Lk. 16:27. Based on the craving for better evidence than the Word of God. We are saved by faith in the Word, not apparitions. The latter lead men into darkness.

Spiritualism. 1 Sam. 28. Saul and the witch. To think any spiritualistic medium can be of help when God has frowned upon us is to heap contempt upon God, who has expressly forbidden such intercourse. V. 14 is either a real appearance, allowed by God to announce Saul's doom to him, or a pretended appearance due to evil spirit. Seems to be real here, for Samuel came not at the woman's behest (note her fright and astonishment) but by Jehovah's command. Importance of the crisis in the affairs of Saul and the nation would seem sufficient reason for Jehovah's actions. Note v. 8. Saul sneaks to a spiritist at night. Such works are of the darkness.

Stewards—Handling of money for God's work, 2 Kgs. 12. Those so entrusted must learn to deal faithfully. God will reckon with them if they do

not. Loose financial methods in the
church dishonor God.

Stewardship—Christian. Acts 4:32.
The stewardship here taught is not the
modern socialist doctrine of the aboli-
tion of the rights of property.

Substitutionary Atonement. Gen. 4:
1-7. **Attainment** cannot be substitute
for **atonement**. Cain refuses to own
himself a lost sinner and tries to approach God on ground of nature. Abel
takes God at His word (Heb. 11:4;
Lev. 17:1), places death of another between himself and consequences of his
sin. Christ, the spotless victim.

Suffering—for Christ's sake. Acts
9:16. Those who do most for God are
often called to suffer most. See 2 Cor.
1:3-11; 11:24-30; Phil. 1:29; Col. 1:24.

Talents — Recognition of our. 2
Chron. 9. Best way to get the credit
of our endowments, as well as full en-
joyment of them, is to consecrate them
to God and use them for Him.

Temperate living. Dan 1. Plain
living and high thinking go together.
God's people should not set affections

on the delights of sense, but should look upon them with indifference.

Temptation—Deliverance in. Mt. 4. Word of God is sword of the Spirit, which, if rightly handled, will deal defeat to Satan. Beware of Satan's twisting of Scripture when you use the Word against him.

Temptation in weak moments. Jn. 18: 17. How easily Satan gets in. Peter made a speedy surrender at the slightest attack from a little girl's tongue.

Temptation—Satan's methods of. Lk. 4. Uses the Word of God. When he could not tempt Christ away from the Word, he tried to tempt Him by the Word. Note his misquotation of it (v. 10; cf. Ps. 91:11).

Testimony—Christian. Gen. 35:1-5. When one enters path of testimony with sense of personal weakness and leaning on God, he has power with men. When testimony becomes force of habit, without simple dependence, it loses its power.

Testimony for Christ. Jn. 9. Criticism of Christ to one who had been hailed by him, opened the way for a clean-cut testimony. Christ's work often occasions gossip. Note this man's full (v. 11, 15, 17, 25), frank (v. 27) and faithful (v. 30, 34) testimony.

Testimony of faith. 1 Kgs. 18. Elijah the man of faith is not afraid to risk his all on the honor of God (v. 23). Let opposers who scoff at testimony of Christians, do what Christianity can do —bring down the cleansing, consuming, illuminating power of God into the lives of men.

Testimony—Paul's. Acts 22. When enemies rage against Christianity, a Christian can offer no better defense than to relate his own vital experience with the saving power of Christ.

Testing—Means of awakening conscience. Gen. 42. Joseph's guilty brothers take thought of their past sins when deep trouble comes.

Testing of believers. Gen. 12:10-20. After communion with God (v. 7-8) may expect faith to be tested. Some go down into Egypt rather than set up altar of worship and faith.

Testings of faith. Ruth 1. Elimelech and family abandon land of favor and sojourn in Moab because testing comes. Better trust in God in Canaan than be punished in Moab with plenty. Moab place of divine displeasure (Deut. 23:3). Writer of Ruth shows that calamities which befell Elimelech and family were because they did not stay in the land of God's favor and trust Him.

Testing—Purpose of. Job 1 and throughout. Trial as the school of faith—not always given as chastisement but to sift our motives and make us more like the Master. In Job's case it was proved that there was more in him than was attached to him.

Thankfulness for blessings through Christ. Lk. 17:11-19. Only one of ten thought of Christ's love—nine thought only of His power. The thanks of the one were as specific as his prayers.

Thankfulness — Remembrance of God's deliverances. Ex. 13. Value of observances to impress it on the heart. Under the Gospel, Christ said, "This do in remembrance of me."

Thankfulness. Remembrance of past blessings. 1 Sam. 7:12. Christian should, as he passes along, set up his Ebenezers, by which he will be reminded that "hitherto the Lord hath helped him."

Thoughtfulness of others. Jn. 12:1-8. Break your alabaster boxes while your friend can enjoy them. Better a plain coffin and no flowers or eulogy, than a life without broken alabaster boxes.

Traitors to Christ. Mk. 14:19. A Judas is hidden in all of us. Beware of him. There is safety in often asking, "Is it I?"

Translation of saints. Enoch, seventh from Adam, made trophy of God's power over death, Gen. 5:24; cf. 1 Cor. 15:51, 52; 1 Thess. 1:10. Note how little influence Enoch's translation had on world.

Trial—Cause of. Cf. Jonah 1 and Acts 27:21. Much depends upon the way we come into trouble. Jonah on the ship was a cause of disaster because out of God's will. Paul on a ship in storm was source of hope.

Trial. Gen. 15:17. Smoking furnace picture of trials through which believer is to pass in coming to his inheritance. The lighted lamp tells of God's relief which shines brighter as the road gets darker.

Trial—Perseverance in. Job 13. Job perseveres in the way of duty though it costs him all that is dear in the world. Do we rejoice in God when we have nothing else to rejoice in?

Trial—Purpose of God in. Job 42. Job, a man whose outward life was blameless, becomes the most troubled man. God deals with his inner life. The answer shows the trials were not for something Job had done but for what he was. Had not the sentence of death in himself (see ch. 29). A good man but too much aware of it. He passes from a knowledge about God to a knowledge of God. Sees God and gets the humbling vision of self. The valley of humbling—a blessed place.

Trials. Ex. 15:23-26. Bitter waters in the path of God's leading, speak of the trials that come to God's people for their edification, not punishment. The cross cast into the bitter waters will make them sweet. (v. 25; Gal. 3:13).

Trials—The succession of. Acts 23-

28. It never rains but it pours. The mysterious law of succession in troubles. God keeps them up until His purpose has been accomplished.

Trials—Trusting God cheerfully in. Acts 27. Since God has promised to be faithful to His own in the storms, let them be cheerful, knowing while He has work for them to do, no difficulty can get in the way.

Trinity—The. Mt. 3. Manifested at baptism of Jesus.

Trouble—Deliverance from. Jonah 2. Though we bring trouble on ourselves by sidestepping God's will, and have to go down to the bottom, if we pray in sincerity, God will speak the word of deliverance.

Trusting God—in danger. Ex. 14. Faith's first attitude in presence of trial is to "stand still." Can't go ahead in divine strength till we have learned to stand still in our own helplessness and look to God.

Two Natures (of believer). Gen. 8. Raven and dove. Raven represents the "old man" satisfied with a world under judgment. Dove the "new man" finding satisfaction only in things of new creation.

Unbelief—Boasting of. 1 Sam. 17: 42-49. Goliath's big words. Unbelief boasts, faith believes. Unbelief looks about (v. 43), faith looks up. "Am I a dog?"—note v. 49 where God proves to him that he was little better than a dog.

Unbelief—Found even in best saints. Jn. 11. Note Jesus' promises—v. 4, 15, 23, 25. Note the slowness of belief in His word, v. 21, 32, 33, 37, 39. Why did Jesus weep? May it not have been because His closest friends hesitated to trust Him fully?

Unbelief. Esau, the man of the earth. Gen. 25:24-34. See Heb. 12:16, 17. Though in some ways nobler than Jacob, he was destitute of faith, despising his birthright because it was a spiritual thing.

Unbelief. Ex. 4. Moses slow to believe God because he cannot find in self a reason for believing. Slow to venture on naked promise of God.

Unbelief. Gen. 20. Abraham lowers himself before world by losing sense of

God's sufficiency for every emergency. Unbelief may lead child of God to moral degradation.

Unbelief. Gen. 16. Sarah gets eyes off God and resorts to device of unbelief, which only brought trouble in home. God could do nothing for her until wrongs had been righted and trust was fully in Him.

Unbelief—How to deal with. Acts 12:16. Way to treat unbelief is just to keep hammering away at the door.

Unbelief. Num. 13-14. Israel fearing the giants in the land. Uneasiness that arises from doubt. Giants cannot stand in way of Christ's work if His people will be valiant in His strength.

Unbelief. 1 Sam. 21. David fails to trust God and resorts to miserable and dishonoring devices for his own preservation in times of testing. Temptation to take things into our own hands when under testing.

Unbelievers—Perilous position of. Ex. 14:23-27. The waters were safe for those who walked by faith, but scoffers who attempted to imitate faith's actings were confounded.

Unitarianism—Sure cure for. Mt.
14:22-36. Deity of Christ will be proved
to anyone who is out on a boisterous
sea where no human power can help,
and then seeing Him come forth to
quiet the winds and save the sinking
soul. "Of a truth thou art the Son of
God."

Unitarians. Mk. 2:6-9. Scribes here
use the Unitarian argument. Jesus
proves to them His own deity by speaking the word of forgiveness and healing.

Victory—Best means of. 1 Sam. 26.
No questionable means need be employ-
ed to help out God's plans for our advancement (v. 10). Wait God's time.
He can weaken the strongest and befool
the wisest on our behalf.

Victory—for God's people. Josh. 8.
Believer, clad in whole armor of God,
meeting enemy as God directs—the
scales turned against those who do not
have God on their side.

Victory in Christ's cause. Josh. 10.
When enemies threaten to swallow up
the church may apply to our Joshua,
the giver of victory. See v. 25. Figure

of Christ's victories over the powers of darkness and the believer's victories through Him.

Victory of faith. David defeats Goliath. 1 Sam. 17. The battle is God's. If confidence is in God's power rather than any armor of sufficiency of our own, world's utmost might cannot stand. God can humiliate the proud by defeating them with the meanest of instruments.

Victory of faith in whatever crisis. 1 Sam. 14. Jonathan and his armor-bearer count on God and ignore obstacles. No matter how few and feeble those who look to God for direction and acknowledge Him in all their ways, God will give the victory. Let faith venture out on His promises.

Victory—Thankfulness for. Esther 9:19. Thanksgiving and alms-giving go well together. If we as a people have received great mercy, the best way to express gratitude is to show mercy.

Vision—The need of. 2 Kgs. 6:13-17. Elisha prayed not for help but for eye-opener. Need eyes open to God's grace (v. 17) and to God's judgment (v.

20). Christian on his knees can see more than philosopher on his tiptoes.

Vows—Caution in making. Judges 11. Jephthah's awful vow. Be cautious and well advised in making vows, lest by indulging a present emotion, even of pious zeal, we involve ourselves and others in a great mistake.

Waiting God's time. 1 Sam. 26. David resorts to no questionable means to hasten his own advancement but waits God's time and way, and with greater results in the end.

War—Sometimes ordered of God. 1 Kgs. 20:35-43. There are times when keeping back the sword from blood is doing the work of God deceitfully. Foolish piety has spoiled many a victory.

Wastefulness—Sin of. Jn. 6:1-13. If we waste what Jesus gives us, He will bring us to want (v. 12, 13). The wasted fragments would evangelize the world.

Watchfulness in prayer. Neh. 4:13. Having prayed, they set a watch. We cannot secure ourselves by prayer without watchfulness, Mt. 26:41.

Wife—Power over husband. 1 Kgs. 22:25, 26. Wife brings out the worst or the best there is in a man.

Will of God. Gen. 12. God bidding Abram to go forth not knowing whither. Testing in the path to which we are called not an evidence we are out of His will. Path of obedience may be trying to flesh.

Will of God. Gen. 13:1-3. When we sidestep God's plan for our lives, like Abram we eventually have to go back to the place we left off.

Will of God—Missing the. 2 Chron. 26:15-17. Uzziah kills his career by undertaking something God has never called him to do. To play the priest when uncalled is to play with fire.

Will of God—Permissive and absolute. Gen. 46. God's absolute will was for the covenant family to be in Canaan (Gen. 26:1-5). He had forbidden Egypt to them, yet now out of tenderness to the broken Jacob, gives a promise of His blessing in Egypt. God follows His people and blesses so far as possible even when they are out of His best. Highest blessing only in obedience to His absolute will.

Will of God—Running ahead of. Ex. 2:11-25. Moses runs ahead of God's plans, gets himself in trouble and suffers a long set-back.

Will of God—Safety in. Mk. 4:37-39. No unexpected storm can defeat God's counsels. If doing His will, He is in the boat.

Will of God—Trifling with. Gen. 27. Nature plotting to bring about what the divine purpose would have brought about without any scheming. Taking ourselves out of God's hands brings sorrow.

Will of God—Working of. Acts 28. Paul is thrown up by the waves on the shore of a strange land, there to do the will of God. Rom. 8:28. An ill wind that blows nobody good.

Wisdom—Solomon an illustration of. 1 Kgs. 3. God's wisdom is laid up for those having spirit of a child (v. 7-9). See Lk. 10:21. Necessity of feeling own insufficiency. Wisdom an object for prayer (v. 9; Jas. 1:5).

Witness—Humble. Their part in

God's great program. "Little maid" —2 Kgs. 5. World brought to God, not alone by Elishas in the pulpits but by "little maids" witnessing outside. But for her Naaman wouldn't have been healed.

Witnessing — Fearlessness in. Acts 4:13-22. There is a time to be stubborn, when you know you are doing God's will. It is a big service to the devil when a mouth can be stopped from witnessing for Christ.

Witnessing for Christ. Mk. 5:1-20. Those who have been delivered from Satanic power so that they may go in peace should go to witness of His power and grace.

Witnessing. Gen. 6-7. Noah, typical witness and workman. Preached God-given message. One hundred years without convert. Proved his own belief by building ark.

Witnessing—Opposition to. Acts 13:3-13. Those called by the Holy Ghost may venture against the devil's assaults, for the Spirit is with them to give success to the word preached.

Witnessing—Qualifications for. Ex. 4. With God the merest stammerer may prove an efficient witness and need not fear for result of message.

Witnessing—The world's opposition to. Acts 4. The more resolute Christ's servants are to witness for Him, the more spiteful the agents of Satan will be. Persecution gives wings to the truth.

Women—Love of. Solomon, 1 Kgs. 11. God appointed one woman for one man. He who thinks one not enough will not be satisfied with two. When our love gets set on the things of the flesh we are on the downhill path, and cannot easily get untangled.

Word of God—Condemning power of. 2 Kgs. 1. Elijah and Ahaziah. Those who will not listen to God's Word for their comfort will eventually be made to listen to it whether they want it or not.

Word of God—Condemning to the world. Ark, 1 Sam. 6, as a type of the Word. Word in the hands of the world brings them condemnation (v. 2). They seek to get rid of it because loath to part with their sins (v. 4).

Word of God—Greater than men. Acts 12:20-25. Herod gave up the ghost—v. 23. Word of God grew and multiplied—v. 24.

Word of God—Jesus in. Acts 8 :34-37. Can begin anywhere in the Bible and preach Jesus.

Word of God—Our Counsellor. 1 Chron. 13. David errs by consulting leaders instead of the book of Exodus. Multitude of advisers can't take place of Bible. God is unaffected by our majorities.

Word of God—Sowing. Mt. 13 :1-23. Note failure of three-fourths of seed sown, occurred before it had taken root. The test of genuine aceptance. Jas. 2 : 18; Jn. 15 :5.

Worldliness—Cost of. Gen. 19. Lot, a worldly child of God, not permitted to perish but suffers loss of all things. Better to be drawn out of world by joys of heaven than driven out by sorrows of earth. Lost testimony (v. 14).

Worldliness. Ex. 16. Heart has to be weaned from the things of Egypt (world) before it can find any satisfaction in feeding on the wilderness Bread (Christ, bread of life). Why some have no appetite for things of Christ and murmur continually.

Worldliness. Gen. 13:12. Lot a picture of professing Christian trying to make the best of both worlds.

Worldliness. Josh. 8. Achan, caught with forbidden spoil, like those who hold to treasures of the world. He lost the spoil, his life and all. No profit to believer to have worldly riches unless given of God. Those who refrained from the accursed things were entrusted by God. Forbear what God forbids and He will give us treasures with His blessings.

Worldliness. Moab a type of world. Ruth 1. Naomi had no influence for God while in Moab—too full of bitterness (v. 6). Moment she starts back to the land of favor she begins to draw others toward God's land.

Worldliness. Num. 32. Reubenites, Gadites and half tribe of Manasseh, choose their inheritance just outside the land. Christians who choose their portion on the borders of the world—carnal Christians, guided by lust of eye and pride of life.

Worldliness. 1 Sam. 8. Israelites want to live like the world and have organization like the world. Not God's will for them to have a king at this time, but He gives them the answer to their selfish prayers with judgment thrown in. Christian who wants to walk like the world will find himself a dupe at last. 1 Jn. 2:17; Jas. 4:4.

Worldly Desires. Num. 11:5. Some in professing church hanker for the onions, leeks and garlic of the world.

Worship. Ex. 25. Tabernacle. Man has to approach God in appointed way. A righteous God and a ruined sinner may meet (v. 22) on a blood-sprinkled platform and have fellowship (1 Pet. 1: 18, 19). Tabernacle foreshadows Christ. Gold, a type of deity, silver of redemption, brass of judgment, blue of heavenly origin, purple of royalty, scarlet of atonement, etc.

Worship—False. Lev. 10. Strange fire of Nadab and Abihu speaks of the use of carnal means to kindle the fires of devotion and praise, which, if true, come only from Christ and the Holy Spirit. Danger of leading people without getting God's mind (Col. 2:23).

Worship—Fleshly. 1 Kgs. 12:25-33. Men always seeking improved plans of worship, something easier on the conscience. Jeroboam would be called a "liberal." Note in v. 28 he tries to give impression it is the same old religion, only a modernized way of stating it.

Worship—Hindrances to. Lev. 2: 11. Leaven forbidden. Leaven in Scripture a type of malice, wickedness and human pride. Spoils all spiritual sacrifices. Beware of sins which spoil acceptableness of worship.

Youth—Service in. 2 Chron. 34:3. Josiah didn't have to sow his wild oats but entered active service for God.

To a student of the Bible Institute of Los Angeles, I am indebted for the idea of this work, which I dedicate to the students of the Institute, praying that it may be a tool in their hands which will ever remind them of the exhortation of a great preacher—"Preach the Word."